IDENTITY

IDENTITY

Essays Based on Herbert Spencer Lectures Given in the University of Oxford

Edited by

HENRY HARRIS

Sometime Regius Professor of Medicine, Oxford

CLARENDON PRESS · OXFORD
1995

Oxford University Press, Walton Street, Oxford OX2 6DP
Oxford New York
Athens Auckland Bangkok Bombay
Calcutta Cape Town Dar es Salaam Delhi
Florence Hong Kong Istanbul Karachi
Kuala Lumpur Madras Madrid Melbourne
Mexico City Nairobi Paris Singapore
Taipei Tokyo Toronto
and associated companies in
Berlin Ibadan

Oxford is a trade mark of Oxford University Press

Published in the United States
by Oxford University Press Inc., New York

British Library Cataloguing-in-Publication Data
Data available

Library of Congress Cataloging in Publication Data

Identity: essays based on Herbert Spencer lectures given in the University of
Oxford / edited by Henry Harris.
Includes bibliographical references and index.
1. Identity (Psychology) 2. Gender identity. 3. Group identity.
I. Harris, Henry, 1925– . II. Series: Herbert Spencer lecture.
BF697.I345 1995 126—dc20 94-38255

ISBN 0-19-823525-9

1 3 5 7 9 10 8 6 4 2

Typeset by Best-set Typesetter Ltd., Hong Kong
Printed in Great Britain
on acid-free paper by
Bookcraft (Bath) Ltd.
Midsomer Norton, Avon

PREFACE

Although the English language is rich in synonyms, there are some words that are islands of desperate poverty in this respect. 'Identity' is one of them. It stands in for so many different concepts that to use it at all is a recipe for confusion. There is, first, the canonical philosophical distinction between 'qualitative' and 'numerical' identity. If, of two objects, it can be said that any property whatsoever that one of them has, the other also has, then they are said to be qualitatively identical; but it takes no more than a moment's thought to see that no two material objects in the real world are, or could possibly be, of this kind. The identity that engages the attention of modern philosophers is numerical identity, that is, whether, and under what circumstances, one can say that two phenomena observed at different times are one and the same thing. In this volume, Williams sets out the ground rules for the philosophical analysis of this problem and brings to light the intrinsic elements of indeterminacy that the notion of numerical identity entails. Parfit is primarily concerned with 'personal identity', which he explores by a series of science fictions in which personal identity is extended by replication or dissected by transplantation of brains and bodies. Parfit agrees with Williams that there are situations where it cannot be decided whether personal identity has been preserved, but concludes that from a practical (and ultimately moral) point of view the preservation of personal identity is unimportant. Harris argues that defining personal identity is simply a matter of defining what one chooses to call a person, and that fictional devices involving replication of persons or transplantation of brains are not only based on physiological mis-conceptions, but are also seriously misleading. For Harris, all questions of identity in the world of sticks and stones are empirical questions that can be answered, if at all, then only by empirical methods. Ruse does a great deal to clarify the obscure and emotionally charged concept of sexual identity. He offers a critical and biologically informed analysis of the genetic, physiological, and psychological determinants of homosexuality, and he discusses how far it is reasonable to claim that homosexuality is a social construct. Cave takes the view that personal identity is generated through narrative, either the narrative that one weaves about oneself or about other people, both real and fictional. In particular, he examines the crucial role that false identity and its exposure have played in literature from remote antiquity to the present day. Finally, Smith describes the various ways in which national identities are formed and analyses how this process is shaped by the interplay of cultural inheritance, political expediency, and myth. There are, of course, other concepts for which the word identity does duty; but this collection of essays, written by expert hands, covers a good deal of ground. Herbert Spencer would surely have been very pleased with them.

Oxford   H.H.
Michaelmas 1993

CONTENTS

LIST OF FIGURES

LIST OF CONTRIBUTORS

Bernard Williams is White's Professor of Moral Philosophy at Oxford, and Deutsch Professor of Philosophy at the University of California, Berkeley. His principal contributions to philosophy have been in ethics, but he has also written on personal identity, on questions in the theory of knowledge, and on the history of philosophy. He was chairman of the government Committee on Obscenity and Film Censorship, which reported in 1979. He is a Fellow of the British Academy. His publications include *Problems of the Self, Moral Luck, Ethics and the Limits of Philosophy*, and *Shame and Necessity*.

Derek Parfit is a Senior Research Fellow at All Souls College, Oxford. His main publication is *Reasons and Persons* (Oxford University Press, 1984). His recent work on personal identity will appear in *Parfit and his Critics*, edited by Jonathan Dancy (Blackwells, forthcoming).

Henry Harris is Regius Professor of Medicine Emeritus at Oxford. He has made many contributions to cell biology, but is perhaps best known for his introduction of the technique of cell fusion to provide new approaches to the genetic analysis of somatic cells and for his discovery of tumour suppressor genes. He is a Fellow of the Royal Society, a Foreign Honorary Member of the American Academy of Arts and Sciences, a Foreign Member of the Max Planck Society, and an Honorary Fellow of the Cambridge Philosophical Society. His publications include *Nucleus and Cyto-*

plasm, *Cell Fusion*, *The Balance of Improbabilities*, and some fiction.

Michael Ruse is Professor in the Department of Philosophy and Zoology at the University of Guelph. He has edited and written several books, including *Taking Darwin Seriously* and *The Darwinian Paradigm*. Professor Ruse is currently completing his work on Progress and a book on *Evolutionary Naturalism*. He is a Fellow of the Royal Society of Canada and received an Honorary Doctorate from the University of Bergen, and also received the Isaac Walton Killam Fellowship. He is founder and editor of *Biology and Philosophy* and is on the editorial board of *Zygon*, *Philosophy of Science*, and the *Quarterly Review of Biology*.

Terence Cave is Professor of French Literature in the University of Oxford and Fellow of St John's College, Oxford. His publications include *Devotional Poetry in France c.1570–1613* (Cambridge University Press, 1969); *The Cornucopian Text: Problems of Writing in the French Renaissance* (Clarendon Press, 1979); *Recognitions: A Study in Poetics* (Clarendon Press, 1988); and a new translation of Mme de Lafayette's *La Princesse de Clèves* and other stories (World's Classics, Oxford University Press, 1992). He is a fellow of the British Academy, a member of the Academia Europaea, and an Honorary Senior Research Fellow of the Institute of Romance Studies, University of London.

Anthony D. Smith is Professor of Sociology at the London School of Economics. Educated at Wadham College, Oxford, he has doctorates from the University of London in Sociology and in the History of Art. He has taught at the Universities of York and Reading. His publications include *Theories of Nationalism* (Duckworth, 1971; second edition 1983); *The Concept of Social Change* (RKP, 1973); *Nationalism in the Twentieth Century* (Martin Robertson, 1979); *The Ethnic*

Revival (Cambridge University Press, 1981); *State and Nation in the Third World* (Harvester, 1983); *The Ethnic Origins of Nations* (Blackwell, 1986); *National Identity* (Penguin, 1991).

Identity and Identities

BERNARD WILLIAMS

In 1955, there appeared an ingenious and enjoyable novel by Nigel Dennis called *Cards of Identity*. It introduced an organization called the 'Identity Club', which engaged in making people over, giving them a new past and a new character—a new identity. There was much discussion of the *name* that any given character should have. This gives the flavour:

'Has he been with us for long?'

'A good many years. He came straight here from the Navy. I found him, dead-drunk, in a Portsmouth gutter.'

'And he likes his name?'

'He took to it immediately. Would you care to construe?'

'I should love to. We begin with the premise that every butler believes he was born to command a fleet.'

'That is correct. Go on.'

'Nelson, you felt, was too common a name . . . But in Jellicoe you found *everything*—a bellicose, echoing, challenging suggestion discreetly balanced by an opening syllable indicative of a nature congealed and wobbly. In short, though he is for ever partly something pink, shaking guiltily on a plate, he has, in whole, the stuff of leadership.'

'That is first-class, Beaufort. Thus it was, exactly. Incidentally, it may interest you to know that at first I toyed with the idea of an identity from the race-course. But when I put out a few racy feelers, he shrank in horror. That is an important thing to know, by the way. Never, except in rare cases, build on the existing disguise. Imagine the horror of this wretched man if I had taken up his crop and cord breeches and named him Donoghue.'

'And *too* Irish,' murmured Mrs Mallet sleepily. 'Not the streak we want here at the moment, with so much to do.' (Dennis 1955: 40–1)

In this connection 'giving him a new identity' means making him a certain *sort* of person. Although he is not merely an imperious butler, but an imperious butler called Jellicoe, born in a certain town on a certain day, and so forth, this is still a type, though a very individuated type. Underlying the type, in the sense of the identity that is applied to a particular human being, we have the idea of that human being, and his particular identity. The person who gets the new identity in the type-sense still has his old identity in the particular sense: he is, unchangeably, the same human being as the one who was found in the gutter and was made into a dignified butler by the Identity Club.

Many philosophical problems about identity concern the criteria for the identity of particular things. In the first part of this essay I shall consider a number of different philosophical problems that are associated with the concept of the identity of a particular thing. This leads to a particularly important case of the relation of particulars to types, which I shall take up in the later part of the essay: this is the notion of a person's social identity.

I start with more strictly metaphysical questions. Identity intimately involves counting, either synchronic or over time, and problems of identity are connected with what, in ancient terms, may be called questions of the One and the Many, of how many things of a certain sort there are at a certain place or over a certain period. As Frege helpfully insisted, the question 'how many?' always demands an answer to 'how many what?' What we have in front of us may be one wood and 500 trees, or one library and 2,000 books. In these cases, the more numerous things, the trees or books, constitute, make up, or are parts of the one thing, and the one thing indeed looks like an aggregate of particular things. But sometimes, the one may be a great deal more obvious than the many. This is a significant point in biology. There are many species of animals, for instance jellyfish of the order *Siphonophora*, such as the notorious Portuguese man-of-war, with which the manifest individual is, in fact, a colony of smaller and rather different individuals joined together: there is one Portuguese man-of-war, which is a colony or association of many constituent animals. Since the colonial participants may be functionally differentiated to some extent, this raises questions about the boundaries of an individual, and also what counts as a biological type. With the Portuguese man-of-war, it is not quite the case that one jellyfish consists of many jellyfish, and quite certainly it does not consist of many Portuguese men-of-war. In other cases, however, the one and the many may collect the same name.

This is characteristic of cloning. There is a species of desert bush that grows in an increasing circle, and parts in the middle, and parts between clumps on the circumference, then die off. This process can yield a circle, in some cases a very large circle, of separate bushes which are in a sense one bush. Is the result one bush with spatially separated parts, or several bushes? In this case it may not matter much. It is easy to answer that it is both one and many, or that it does not matter which one says. But one should not get too attached to the description in terms of 'one thing'. It can run into real difficulties, particularly when we are concerned with motile species. Identity questions typically and unsurprisingly sharpen up when things can move about.

This is obvious in the case of the amoeba. The amoeba divides, and it is extremely important that its division constitutes a form of (asexual) reproduction; the function of this process is to produce two amoebae. If there are two amoebae, then they are not each identical with the one that was there in the first place. If they were identical with that, they would be identical with each other, which means that there would be only one amoeba. This would yield the discouraging result that however hard the amoeba reproduced, it would

3

never increase the population of amoebae. There would simply be parts of the amoeba which turned up in different places. We have good reason to resist this description.

Splitting may look like a particularly good way of preserving one's identity through time. If I could split, it might seem that I would not only go on existing, but do so twice over. But in fact, division is typically destructive of identity through time. The amoeba does not appear in two places at once, but rather gives up its existence so that there will be two amoebae.

An equally ancient metaphysical puzzle concerns form and matter. This in fact leads back quite soon to the One and the Many, and a case in which we end up with more things than we wanted. The fact that a thing of one kind can be made up of or consist of parts or pieces of stuff means, familiarly enough, that the parts can change while the whole remains the same. In the case of creatures, such as ourselves, which consist of living cells which are almost all replaced over a periodic cycle, some find it tempting to say that 'we are not really the same' at the end of this period. This is simply not correct, for a reason which shows that the phenomenon in itself does not yield a puzzle. A living body may be a thing made of cells, without its being the case that the same body is a thing made of the same cells. All that follows is that the same body is the same thing made of cells. The puzzles come not from this in itself, but from cases that involve peculiar items, or again ordinary items that have peculiar histories. A paradigm of identity through time is provided, as so often in philosophy, by standard physical objects, the sort of thing that J. L. Austin used to call 'middle sized dry goods'. There are many sorts of things which by comparison with those material objects are peculiar with respect to identity. They have a history and some sort of location but their criteria of identity seem to be vague or stipulative: there are things such as clubs, regiments, rivers, and so forth. In these cases, it is very obvious that the parts or constituents change, but vague what counts as continuity. Regiments merge, clubs cease and revive, and there are related questions of what counts as their existing at all. Items of these sorts may even be thought to have discontinuous existence, an idea which from a logical point of view is quite awkward. The river dries up for a bit or, like rivers in Australia, regularly dries up for long periods. Is there then no river? Or a dried-up river?

It is not a sign of good sense to make too much of such questions. I do not mean by that, as scientists and others may be disposed to think, that it is philosophy but not good sense; I mean that it is not philosophical good sense. But it is not always easy to rest on the point of conventional decision. As we saw before, with regard to the bush and the amoeba, identity questions can move very quickly from the seemingly trivial and verbal to the genuinely puzzling, and this fact itself is revealing. It is only what is on the surface of how we speak that can be easily rearranged.

An example of this is provided by the famous ship of Theseus, a vessel in which the hero is supposed to have come back to Athens, and which was preserved, but had its constituent planks replaced gradually over a long time until none of the original material remained. This gave rise in ancient times to a question of whether the end-product was the original ship. Thomas Hobbes brilliantly introduced into this not very interesting puzzle the further idea that the original planks were kept and then reassembled into a ship exactly like the original, with the result that there were then two candidates for being the ship of Theseus.[1] As Hobbes pointed out, and as we may recall from the case of the amoeba, they could not both be that particular ship. In the case of the amoeba, it had two descendants both of which arrived by exactly the same means; in the case of the ship, it might be said that there were two descendants which had arrived by different means, that of form and that of matter.

Rather than asking which, if either, is the original ship, it may be more interesting to ask the following question: if

---

[1] *de Corpore* 2. 11. I am indebted on this question to David Wiggins: see Wiggins 1980: 92.

either of these things had existed without the other, would that have been the ship of Theseus? This suggests the idea that the answer to such identity questions is to be given in terms of the best available candidate. In these terms, the continuously repaired ship will indeed be the original if the planks have not been retained and reassembled, but equally the ship made of the original planks would, if the other had been destroyed, be that original ship. This seems, in its own way, quite sensible, but there is something counter-intuitive about Best Candidate Theory.[2] It leads to the result that something can stop being, or become, exactly the same thing as an original item. The ship which Hobbes regarded as the winner—the one made of the original boards—was the worse candidate when it was not even a ship, but a pile of boards. When they were reassembled into a ship, did the other one cease to be the ship of Theseus? Moreover, if there is a contest between two items which results in a tie, this can lead to a merely arbitrary choice of one item to be the original thing. I think that a theory in these terms is a recognizable account of something, but not of numerical identity. What we should rather say about Hobbes's example is that the description 'the ship of Theseus' refers not to a particular ship but to a *role*, rather like the role of the Admiral's flagship; as in that case, the role can be discharged by various particular ships at different times.

The type of example for which Best Candidate Theory is particularly implausible is personal identity. Imaginary or science fiction cases are often discussed in this connection, in which one person's memory and character end up in another person's body, and the question is raised whether the person with Smith's memory and character (the psychological continuant) or the person with Smith's body (the bodily continuant) is Smith. In such a case, Best Candidate Theory seems absurd. From the outside, indeed, we might seem to be left just with a decision whether to say that the bodily continuant

---

[2] It is defended (under the name 'Closest Continuer Theory') by Robert Nozick (1981, ch. 1).

was indeed Smith who had lost his memories and so forth, or alternatively to say that the psychological continuant was Smith in a different body. But from the inside—that it is say from the perspective of the original Smith—it can scarcely seem like a matter of conventional decision. If unpleasant treatment, for instance, is to be applied after such a change to *this* body (the body that the original Smith originally has), should he or should he not expect to be hurt? It is hard to see how the answer to that question could depend upon what decision an observer might arrive at under Best Candidate Theory.

Conventionalism about identity is very tempting, as we saw with the bush, and the regiment, and the river, and the ship of Theseus discussed in antiquity. But faced with Hobbes's two ships of Theseus, and indeed with the amoeba, we are brought to see that conventionalism about identity does not come cheap, and that we have more commitments than we may suppose to dividing the world up on some lines rather than on others. When, further, it comes to myself and the proposed torture, conventionalism seems to lose its grip entirely. Here, conventionalism and Best Candidate Theory seem not to offer an invitation, but merely to demand that we understand our own thoughts better.

Questions at this level about persons are, in a metaphysical sense, questions what or who a person is. Such questions can themselves be related to ethics and politics, in a number of ways. They can bear, for instance, on the ethics and politics of euthanasia. But there is another kind of ethical and political question that can be expressed by asking the question 'what am I?' This kind of question concerns one's identity as a person who belongs to a certain family, group, or race; they are questions of social identity.

In these connections 'identity' has a sense which, as in Nigel Dennis's story, relates to a type or a general thing. A gay or lesbian identity, a native American identity, or that of a Lombard as opposed to an Italian, are all type things, because such an identity is shared. Indeed, it is particularly

7

important that it is shared, and an insistence on such an identity is an insistence on the ways in which it is shared. There is something else that it may have in common with Nigel Dennis's identities; it may be constructed. It will not of course be constructed by the intentions of a club, but by social processes; and again in common with Dennis's Identity Club, some of the construction may be demonstrably fictional.

At this point, it is easy to say that social identity is simply a benign self-applied stereotype, one that is favourable, supportive, and applied to oneself, rather than one that is unfavourable and applied to us by others. There is a grain of truth in this, and it reminds us how a negative stereotype may be by political action converted into a positive identity. But this simple account rides over an essential difference. A stereotype deployed against me by others impinges on my self, and if it gets into it, it is an obstacle to my living freely or effectively or in a convinced way. But an identity that I embrace is an aid to living in such ways. The difference between an identity which is mine and which I eagerly recognize as mine, and an identity as what someone else simply assumes me to be, is in one sense all the difference in the world.

But what is it for a general character or role or type to constitute my identity? Here the relations between type and particular individual are crucial. It is very important that an identity of this kind is not my identity in the particular sense. If it were, then if I were separated from the life and allegiances which expressed that identity I would cease to exist. Moreover, if the form of life that embodied that identity were destroyed, the people who possessed it would cease to exist. But it is not so, and to insist that it is not so is not merely a piece of pedantry or an affirmation of abstract metaphysics. The point is included, rather, in the thoughts of the people who have such identities themselves. If those disasters happen, the particular people will still exist, because it is they who will have been damaged or wronged by this happening. If, for instance, native Americans on reservations are conscious of the loss of an identity, they are conscious precisely of *their own* loss. The destruction of a culture is often said to be a kind of genocide, but, while putting it like this has a point, it significantly misplaces the wrong or damage of which it is complaining. The loss of a culture can be seen from a conservationist point of view, as the loss of variety or of a human possibility; but that is an external point of view on it, as it is with the extinction of a species.

An essential part of the idea of social identity is that a particular human being can find or lose identity in social groups. Henri Tajfel, the founder of modern social identity theory, defined social identity as 'the individual's knowledge that he or she belongs to certain social groups together with some emotional or value significance to him or her of the group membership'.[3] This account is enough for many of the questions that are pursued in social psychology under this general title, such as the relations of group membership to self-esteem, perceptions of salience, the relations between in-groups and out-groups, and so on. However, it goes rather wide as a definition of what might be called more strictly an *identity*. Thus someone may be very conscious of his or her membership of MENSA or of the Royal Society, and derive self-esteem from this, without its constituting or powerfully contributing to his or her identity. Indeed, a person who found his or her identity fundamentally in the membership of one of these organizations might be thought to be in a bad way.

One feature of the general or type classification that can help it to contribute to someone's identity is that it is thought to explain or underlie a lot of the individual's activities, emotions, reactions and, in general, life. It is from the point of view of those who endorse it a deep social classification. This in itself, of course, does not make it into a 'sortal' concept— that is to say, a fundamental concept for counting: the number of Quebecois people present is the same as the

---

[3] Quoted in Abrams and Hogg 1990: 2.

number of human beings present who are Quebecois. 'Human being' is, roughly, a term of nature, and 'Quebecois' a term of culture. But for those to whom 'Quebecois' is a powerful term of social identity it is as basic a classificatory term in culture as 'human being' is in nature.

However, it is also typical of such identities that they are not just analogous to the classifications of nature, but closely related to nature. You are, for instance, typically *born* in some relation to Quebec that makes you a Quebecois. When people of some minority cease trying to assimilate and opt for a culturally distinct identity, they seek to affirm an *origin*.

It is not always simply like this. Thus people may find their identity in a religious sect which they voluntary join. But it is typical in such cases that they have some sense that this is not just opting for one group among others but constitutes finding something that was there; or coming home—one kind of obedience to Nietzsche's splendid instruction 'become what you are'. In such a case, though I may feel that I have come there voluntarily, what I have come to lies outside my will: something is given, even though I must choose to take it up. This is true, of course, also of those other cases, of national or racial or tribal identification; the will may be exercised in coming to coincide with something that I already un-changeably am.

This is one reason, also, why there is a special complexity to sexual identity. The self-conscious adoption of a gay or a straight life has its significance, surely, because it is not just joining one or another club but counts as a recognition of something. At the same time, that consciousness requires also that being gay or straight should not just be a matter of genetic or developmental determinism. There must be a space for both nature and the will.

All this helps us, perhaps, to see why the politics of identity should be so essential to our life now. Ever since the Enlightenment a recurrent aspiration of distinctively modern politics has been for a life that is indeed individual, particular, mine, within the reach of my will, yet at the same time expresses more than me, and shapes my life in terms that mean something because they lie beyond the will and are concretely given to me. It is the politics, if you like, of self-realization. That term contains in itself obvious difficulties: it is even grammatically ambiguous between activity and passivity, and illuminatingly so. Those obscurities are the product not of mere semantic inefficiency, but of unresolved political and personal tensions. This is one application of a more general lesson about philosophical problems of identity, that if we find it systematically hard to know what to say, the problem lies probably not in our words but in our world.

2

The Unimportance of Identity

DEREK PARFIT

We can start with some science fiction. Here on Earth, I enter the Teletransporter. When I press some button, a machine destroys my body, while recording the exact states of all my cells. The information is sent by radio to Mars, where another machine makes, out of organic materials, a perfect copy of my body. The person who wakes up on Mars seems to remember living my life up to the moment when I pressed the button, and he is in every other way just like me.

Of those who have thought about such cases, some believe that it would be I who would wake up on Mars. They regard Teletransportation as merely the fastest way of travelling. Others believe that, if I chose to be Teletransported, I would be making a terrible mistake. On their view, the person who wakes up would be a mere Replica of me.

I

That is a disagreement about personal identity. To understand such disagreements, we must distinguish two kinds of sameness. Two white billiard balls may be qualitatively identical, or exactly similar. But they are not numerically ident-

Some of this essay draws from Part Three of my *Reasons and Persons* (Oxford University Press, 1984). The new material will be more fully developed in my contribution to Dancy, *Derek Parfit and His Critics: Vol. I. Persons* (Blackwell's, forthcoming).

ical, or one and the same ball. If I paint one of these balls red, it will cease to be qualitatively identical with itself as it was; but it will still be one and the same ball. Consider next a claim like, 'Since her accident, she is no longer the same person'. That involves both senses of identity. It means that *she*, one and the same person, is *not* now the same person. That is not a contradiction. The claim is only that this person's character has changed. This numerically identical person is now qualitatively different.

When psychologists discuss identity, they are typically concerned with the kind of person someone is, or wants to be. That is the question involved, for example, in an identity crisis. But, when philosophers discuss identity, it is numerical identity they mean. And, in our concern about our own futures, that is what we have in mind. I may believe that, after my marriage, I shall be a different person. But that does not make marriage death. However much I change, I shall still be alive if there will be someone living who will be me. Similarly, if I was Teletransported, my Replica on Mars would be qualitatively identical to me; but, on the sceptic's view, he wouldn't *be* me. *I* shall have ceased to exist. And that, we naturally assume, is what matters.

Questions about our numerical identity all take the following form. We have two ways of referring to a person, and we ask whether these are ways of referring to the same person. Thus we might ask whether Boris Nikolayevich is Yeltsin. In the most important questions of this kind, our two ways of referring to a person pick out a person at different times. Thus we might ask whether the person to whom we are speaking now is the same as the person to whom we spoke on the telephone yesterday. These are questions about identity over time.

To answer such questions, we must know the *criterion* of personal identity: the relation between a person at one time, and a person at another time, which makes these one and the same person.

Different criteria have been advanced. On one view, what makes me the same, throughout my life, is my having the same body. This criterion requires uninterrupted bodily continuity. There is no such continuity between my body on Earth and the body of my Replica on Mars; so, on this view, my Replica would not be me. Other writers appeal to psychological continuity. Thus Locke claimed that, if I was conscious of a past life in some other body, I would be the person who lived that life. On some versions of this view, my Replica would be me.

Supporters of these different views often appeal to cases where they conflict. Most of these cases are, like Teletransportation, purely imaginary. Some philosophers object that, since our concept of a person rests on a scaffolding of facts, we should not expect this concept to apply in imagined cases where we think those facts away. I agree. But I believe that, for a different reason, it is worth considering such cases. We can use them to discover, not what the truth is, but what we believe. We might have found that, when we consider science fiction cases, we simply shrug our shoulders. But that is not so. Many of us find that we have certain beliefs about what kind of fact personal identity is.

These beliefs are best revealed when we think about such cases from a first-person point of view. So, when I imagine something's happening to me, you should imagine its happening to you. Suppose that I live in some future century, in which technology is far advanced, and I am about to undergo some operation. Perhaps my brain and body will be remodelled, or partially replaced. There will be a resulting person, who will wake up tomorrow. I ask, 'Will that person be me? Or am I about to die? Is this the end?' I may not know how to answer this question. But it is natural to assume that there must *be* an answer. The resulting person, it may seem, must be either me, or someone else. And the answer must be all-or-nothing. That person cannot be *partly* me. If that person is in pain tomorrow, this pain cannot be partly mine. So, we may assume, either I shall feel that pain, or I shan't.

If this is how we think about such cases, we assume that our identity must be *determinate*. We assume that, in every imaginable case, questions about our identity must have answers, which must be either, and quite simply, Yes or No.

Let us now ask: 'Can this be true?' There is one view on which it might be. On this view, there are immaterial substances: souls, or Cartesian Egos. These entities have the special properties once ascribed to atoms: they are indivisible, and their continued existence is, in its nature, all or nothing. And such an Ego is what each of us really is.

Unlike several writers, I believe that such a view might have been true. But we have no good evidence for thinking that it is, and some evidence for thinking that it isn't; so I shall assume here that no such view is true.

If we do not believe that there are Cartesian Egos, or other such entities, we should accept the kind of view which I have elsewhere called *Reductionist*. On this view

(1) A person's existence just consists in the existence of a body, and the occurrence of a series of thoughts, experiences, and other mental and physical events.

Some Reductionists claim

(2) Persons just *are* bodies.

This view may seem not to be Reductionist, since it does not reduce persons to something else. But that is only because it is hyper-Reductionist: it reduces persons to bodies in so strong a way that it doesn't even distinguish between them. We can call it *Identifying* Reductionism.

Such a view seems to me too simple. I believe that we should combine (1) with

(3) A person is an entity that has a body, and has thoughts and other experiences.

On this view, though a person is distinct from that person's body, and from any series of thoughts and experiences, the person's existence just *consists* in them. So we can call this view *Constitutive* Reductionism.

16

It may help to have other examples of this kind of view. If we melt down a bronze statue, we destroy this statue, but we do not destroy this lump of bronze. So, though the statue just consists in the lump of bronze, these cannot be one and the same thing. Similarly, the existence of a nation just consists in the existence of a group of people, on some territory, living together in certain ways. But the nation is not the same as that group of people, or that territory.

Consider next *Eliminative* Reductionism. Such a view is sometimes a response to arguments against the Identifying view. Suppose we start by claiming that a nation just is a group of people on some territory. We are then persuaded that this cannot be so: that the concept of a nation is the concept of an entity that is distinct from its people and its territory. We may conclude that, in that case, there are really no such things as nations. There are only groups of people, living together in certain ways.

In the case of persons, some Buddhist texts take an Eliminative view. According to these texts

(4) There really aren't such things as persons: there are only brains and bodies, and thoughts and other experiences.

For example:

Buddha has spoken thus: 'O brethren, actions do exist, and also their consequences, but the person that acts does not. . . . There exists no Individual, it is only a conventional name given to a set of elements.'

Or:

The mental and the material are really here,
But here there is no person to be found.
For it is void and merely fashioned like a doll,
Just suffering piled up like grass and sticks.

Eliminative Reductionism is sometimes justified. Thus we are right to claim that there were really no witches, only persecuted women. But Reductionism about some kind of entity

Derek Parfit

is not often well expressed with the claim that there are no such entities. We should admit that there are nations, and that we, who are persons, exist.

Rather than claiming that there are no entities of some kind, Reductionists should distinguish kinds of entity, or ways of existing. When the existence of an X just consists in the existence of a Y, or Ys, though the X is *distinct* from the Y or Ys, it is not an *independent* or *separately existing* entity. Statues do not exist separately from the matter of which they are made. Nor do nations exist separately from their citizens and their territory. Similarly, I believe,

> (5) Though persons are distinct from their bodies, and from any series of mental events, they are not independent or separately existing entities.

Cartesian Egos, if they existed, would not only be distinct from human bodies, but would also be independent entities. Such Egos are claimed to be like physical objects, except that they are wholly mental. If there were such entities, it would make sense to suppose that they might cease to be causally related to some body, yet continue to exist. But, on a Reductionist view, persons are not in that sense independent from their bodies. (That is not to claim that our thoughts and other experiences are merely changes in the states of our brains. Reductionists, while not believing in purely mental substances, may be dualists.)

We can now return to personal identity over time, or what constitutes the continued existence of the same person. One question here is this. What explains the unity of a person's mental life? What makes thoughts and experiences, had at different times, the thoughts and experiences of a single person? According to some Non-Reductionists, this question cannot be answered in other terms. We must simply claim that these different thoughts and experiences are all had by the same person. This fact does not consist in any other facts, but is a bare or ultimate truth.

18

The unimportance of identity

If each of us was a Cartesian Ego, that might be so. Since such an Ego would be an independent substance, it could be an irreducible fact that different experiences are all changes in the states of the same persisting Ego. But that could not be true of persons, I believe, if, while distinct from their bodies, they are not separately existing entities. A person, so conceived, is not the kind of entity about which there could be such irreducible truths. When experiences at different times are all had by the same person, this fact must consist in certain other facts.

If we do not believe in Cartesian Egos, we should claim

(6) Personal identity over time just consists in physical and/or psychological continuity.

That claim could be filled out in different ways. On one version of this view, what makes different experiences the experiences of a single person is their being either changes in the states of, or at least directly causally related to, the same embodied brain. That must be the view of those who believe that persons just are bodies. And we might hold that view even if, as I think we should, we distinguish persons from their bodies. But we might appeal, either in addition or instead, to various psychological relations between different mental states and events, such as the relations involved in memory, or in the persistence of intentions, desires, and other psychological features. That is what I mean by psychological continuity.

On Constitutive Reductionism, the fact of personal identity is distinct from these facts about physical and psychological continuity. But, since it just consists in them, it is not an independent or separately obtaining fact. It is not a further difference in what happens.

To illustrate that distinction, consider a simpler case. Suppose that I already know that several trees are growing together on some hill. I then learn that, because that is true, there is a copse on this hill. That would not be new factual information. I would have merely learnt that such a group of trees can be called a 'copse'. My only new information is about our language. That those trees can be called a copse is not, except trivially, a fact about the trees.

Something similar is true in the more complicated case of nations. In order to know the facts about the history of a nation, it is enough to know what large numbers of people did and said. Facts about nations cannot be barely true: they must consist in facts about people. And, once we know these other facts, any remaining questions about nations are not further questions about what really happened.

I believe that, in the same way, facts about people cannot be barely true. Their truth must consist in the truth of facts about bodies, and about various interrelated mental and physical events. If we knew these other facts, we would have all the empirical input that we need. If we understood the concept of a person, and had no false beliefs about what persons are, we would then know, or would be able to work out, the truth of any further claims about the existence or identity of persons. That is because such claims would not tell us more about reality.

That is the barest sketch of a Reductionist view. These remarks may become clearer if we return to the so-called 'problem cases' of personal identity. In such a case, we imagine knowing that, between me now and some person in the future, there will be certain kinds or degrees of physical and/or psychological continuity or connectedness. But, though we know these facts, we cannot answer the question whether that future person would be me.

Since we may disagree on which the problem cases are, we need more than one example. Consider first the range of cases that I have elsewhere called the *Physical Spectrum*. In each of these cases, some proportion of my body would be replaced, in a single operation, with exact duplicates of the existing cells. In the case at the near end of this range, no cells would be replaced. In the case at the far end, my whole body would be destroyed and replicated. That is the case with which I began: Teletransportation.

Suppose we believe that in that case, where my whole body would be replaced, the resulting person would not be me, but a mere Replica. If no cells were replaced, the resulting person would be me. But what of the cases in between, where the percentage of the cells replaced would be, say, 30, or 50, or 70 per cent? Would the resulting person here be me? When we consider some of these cases, we will not know whether to answer Yes or No.

Suppose next that we believe that, even in Teletransportation, my Replica would be me. We should then consider a different version of that case, in which the Scanner would get its information without destroying my body, and my Replica would be made while I was still alive. In this version of the case, we may agree that my Replica would not be me. That may shake our view that, in the original version of case, he *would* be me.

If we still keep that view, we should turn to what I have called the *Combined Spectrum*. In this second range of cases, there would be all the different degrees of both physical and psychological connectedness. The new cells would not be exactly similar. The greater the proportion of my body that would be replaced, the less like me would the resulting person be. In the case at the far end of this range, my whole body would be destroyed, and they would make a Replica of some quite different person, such as Greta Garbo. Garbo's Replica would clearly *not* be me. In the case at the near end, with no replacement, the resulting person would be me. On any view, there must be cases in between where we could not answer our question.

For simplicity, I shall consider only the Physical Spectrum, and I shall assume that, in some of the cases in this range, we cannot answer the question whether the resulting person would be me. My remarks could be transferred, with some adjustment, to the Combined Spectrum.

As I have said, it is natural to assume that, even if *we* cannot answer this question, there must always *be* an answer, which must be either Yes or No. It is natural to believe that, if the resulting person will be in pain, either I shall feel that pain, or I shan't. But this range of cases challenges that belief. In the case at the near end, the resulting person would be me. In the case at the far end, he would be someone else. How could it be true that, in all the cases in between, he must be either me, or someone else? For that to be true, there must be, somewhere in this range, a sharp borderline. There must be some critical set of cells such that, if only those cells were replaced, it would be me who would wake up, but that in the very next case, with only just a few more cells replaced, it would be, not me, but a new person. That is hard to believe.

Here is another fact, which makes it even harder to believe. Even if there were such a borderline, no one could ever discover where it is. I might say, 'Try replacing half of my brain and body, and I shall tell you what happens.' But we know in advance that, in every case, since the resulting person would be exactly like me, he would be inclined to believe that he was me. And this could not show that he *was* me, since any mere Replica of me would think that too.

Even if such cases actually occurred, we would learn nothing more about them. So it does not matter that these cases are imaginary. We should try to decide now whether, in this range of cases, personal identity could be determinate. Could it be true that, in every case, the resulting person either would or would not be me?

If we do not believe that there are Cartesian Egos, or other such entities, we seem forced to answer No. It is not true that our identity must be determinate. We can always ask, 'Would that future person be me?' But, in some of these cases,

(7) This question would have no answer. It would be neither true nor false that this person would be me.

And

(8) This question would be *empty*. Even without an answer, we could know the full truth about what happened.

If our questions were about such entities as nations or machines, most of us would accept such claims. But, when applied to ourselves, they can be hard to believe. How could it be neither true nor false that I shall still exist tomorrow? And, without an answer to our question, how could I know the full truth about my future?

Reductionism gives the explanation. We naturally assume that, in these cases, there are different possibilities. The resulting person, we assume, might be me, or he might be someone else, who is merely like me. If the resulting person will be in pain, either I shall feel that pain, or I shan't. If these really were different possibilities, it would be compelling that one of them must be the possibility that would in fact obtain. How could reality fail to choose between them? But, on a Reductionist view,

(9) Our question is not about different possibilities. There is only a single possibility, or course of events. Our question is merely about different possible descriptions of this course of events.

That is how our question has no answer. We have not yet decided which description to apply. And, that is why, even without answering this question, we could know the full truth about what would happen.

Suppose that, after considering such examples, we cease to believe that our identity must be determinate. That may seem to make little difference. It may seem to be a change of view only about some imaginary cases, that will never actually occur. But that may not be so. We may be led to revise our beliefs about the nature of personal identity; and that would be a change of view about our own lives.

In nearly all actual cases, questions about personal identity have answers, so claim (7) does not apply. If we don't know these answers, there is something that we don't know. But claim (8) still applies. Even without answering these questions, we could know the full truth about what happens. We would know that truth if we knew the facts about both physical and psychological continuity. If, implausibly, we still didn't know the answer to a question about identity, our ignorance would only be about our language. And that is because claim (9) still applies. When we know the other facts, there are never different possibilities at the level of what happens. In all cases, the only remaining possibilities are at the linguistic level. Perhaps it would be correct to say that some future person would be me. Perhaps it would be correct to say that he would not be me. Or perhaps neither would be correct. I conclude that in *all* cases, if we know the other facts, we should regard questions about our identity as merely questions about language.

That conclusion can be misunderstood. First, when we ask such questions, that is usually because we *don't* know the other facts. Thus, when we ask if we are about to die, that is seldom a conceptual question. We ask that question because we don't know what will happen to our bodies, and whether, in particular, our brains will continue to support consciousness. Our question becomes conceptual only when we already know about such other facts.

Note next that, in certain cases, the relevant facts go beyond the details of the case we are considering. Whether some concept applies may depend on facts about other cases, or on a choice between scientific theories. Suppose we see something strange happening to an unknown animal. We might ask whether this process preserves the animal's identity, or whether the result is a new animal (because what we are seeing is some kind of reproduction). Even if we knew the details of this process, that question would not be merely conceptual. The answer would depend on whether this process is part of the natural development of this kind of animal. And that may be something we have yet to discover.

If we identify persons with human beings, whom we regard as a natural kind, the same would be true in some imaginable cases involving persons. But these are not the kind of case that I have been discussing. My cases all involve artificial intervention. No facts about natural development could be relevant here. Thus, in my Physical Spectrum, if we knew which of my cells would be replaced by duplicates, all of the relevant empirical facts would be in. In such cases any remaining questions would be conceptual.

Since that is so, it would be clearer to ask these questions in a different way. Consider the case in which I replace some of the components of my audio system, but keep the others. I ask, 'Do I still have one and the same system?' That may seem a factual question. But, since I already know what happened, that is not really so. It would be clearer to ask, 'Given that I have replaced those components, would it be correct to call this the same system?'

The same applies to personal identity. Suppose that I know the facts about what will happen to my body, and about any psychological connections that there will be between me now and some person tomorrow. I may ask, 'Will that person be me?' But that is a misleading way to put my question. It suggests that I don't know what's going to happen. When I know these other facts, I should ask, 'Would it be correct to call that person me?' That would remind me that, if there's anything that I don't know, that is merely a fact about our language.

I believe that we can go further. Such questions are, in the belittling sense, merely verbal. Some conceptual questions are well worth discussing. But questions about personal identity, in my kind of case, are like questions that we would all think trivial. It is quite uninteresting whether, with half its components replaced, I still have the same audio system. In the same way, we should regard it as quite uninteresting whether, if half of my body were simultaneously replaced, I would still exist. As questions about reality, these are entirely empty. Nor, as conceptual questions, do they need answers.

We might need, for legal purposes, to *give* such questions answers. Thus we might decide that an audio system should be called the same if its new components cost less than half its original price. And we might decide to say that I would continue to exist as long as less than half my body were replaced. But these are not answers to conceptual questions; they are mere decisions.

(Similar remarks apply if we are Identifying Reductionists, who believe that persons just are bodies. There are cases where it is a merely verbal question whether we still have one and the same human body. That is clearly true in the cases in the middle of the Physical Spectrum.)

It may help to contrast these questions with one that is not merely verbal. Suppose we are studying some creature which is very unlike ourselves, such as an insect, or some extraterrestrial being. We know all the facts about this creature's behaviour, and its neurophysiology. The creature wriggles vigorously, in what seems to be a response to some injury. We ask, 'Is it conscious, and in great pain? Or is it merely like an insentient machine?' Some Behaviourist might say, 'That is a merely verbal question. These aren't different possibilities, either of which might be true. They are merely different descriptions of the very same state of affairs.' That I find incredible. These descriptions give us, I believe, two quite different possibilities. It could not be an empty or a merely verbal question whether some creature was unconscious or in great pain.

It is natural to think the same about our own identity. If I know that some proportion of my cells will be replaced, how can it be a merely verbal question whether I am about to die, or shall wake up again tomorrow? It is because that is hard to believe that Reductionism is worth discussing. If we become Reductionists, that may change some of our deepest assumptions about ourselves.

These assumptions, as I have said, cover actual cases, and our own lives. But they are best revealed when we consider the imaginary problem cases. It is worth explaining further why that is so.

In ordinary cases, questions about our identity have answers. In such cases, there is a fact about personal identity, and Reductionism is one view about what kind of fact this is. On this view, personal identity just consists in physical and/or psychological continuity. We may find it hard to decide whether we accept this view, since it may be far from clear when one fact just consists in another. We may even doubt whether Reductionists and their critics really disagree.

In the problem cases, things are different. When we cannot answer questions about personal identity, it is easier to decide whether we accept a Reductionist view. We should ask: Do we find such cases puzzling? Or do we accept the Reductionist claim that, even without answering these questions, if we knew the facts about the continuities, we would know what happened?

Most of us do find such cases puzzling. We believe that, even if we knew those other facts, if we could not answer questions about our identity, there would be something that we didn't know. That suggests that, on our view, personal identity does *not* just consist in one or both of the continuities, but is a separately obtaining fact, or a further difference in what happens. The Reductionist account must then leave something out. So there is a real disagreement, and one that applies to all cases.

Many of us do not merely find such cases puzzling. We are inclined to believe that, in all such cases, questions about our identity must have answers, which must be either Yes or No. For that to be true, personal identity must be a separately obtaining fact of a peculiarly simple kind. It must involve some special entity, such as a Cartesian Ego, whose existence must be all-or-nothing.

When I say that we have these assumptions, I am *not* claiming that we believe in Cartesian Egos. Some of us do. But many of us, I suspect, have inconsistent beliefs. If we are asked whether we believe that there are Cartesian Egos, we may answer No. And we may accept that, as Reductionists claim, the existence of a person just involves the existence of a body, and the occurrence of a series of interrelated mental and physical events. But, as our reactions to the problem cases show, we don't fully accept that view. Or, if we do, we also seem to hold a different view.

Such a conflict of beliefs is quite common. At a reflective or intellectual level, we may be convinced that some view is true; but at another level, one that engages more directly with our emotions, we may continue to think and feel as if some different view were true. One example of this kind would be a hope, or fear, that we know to be groundless. Many of us, I suspect, have such inconsistent beliefs about the metaphysical questions that concern us most, such as free will, time's passage, consciousness, and the self.

II

I turn now from the nature of personal identity to its importance. Personal identity is widely thought to have great rational and moral significance. Thus it is the fact of identity which is thought to give us our reason for concern about our own future. And several moral principles, such as those of desert or distributive justice, presuppose claims about identity. The separateness of persons, or the non-identity of different people, has been called 'the basic fact for morals'.

I can comment here on only one of these questions: what matters in our survival. I mean by that, not what makes our survival good, but what makes our survival matter, whether it will be good or bad. What is it, in our survival, that gives us a reason for special anticipatory or prudential concern?

We can explain that question with an extreme imaginary case. Suppose that, while I care about my whole future, I am especially concerned about what will happen to me on future Tuesdays. Rather than suffer mild pain on a future Tuesday, I would choose severe pain on any other future day. That pattern of concern would be irrational. The fact that a pain will be on a Tuesday is no reason to care about it more. What about the fact that a pain will be *mine*? Is *this* a reason to care about it more?

Many people would answer Yes. On their view, what gives us a reason to care about our future is, precisely, that it will be our future. Personal identity is what matters in survival.

I reject this view. Most of what matters, I believe, are two other relations: the psychological continuity and connectedness that, in ordinary cases, hold between the different parts of a person's life. These relations only roughly coincide with personal identity, since, unlike identity, they are in part matters of degree. Nor, I believe, do they matter as much as identity is thought to do.

There are different ways to challenge the importance of identity.

One argument can be summarized like this:

(1) Personal identity just consists in certain other facts.

(2) If one fact just consists in certain others, it can only be these other facts which have rational or moral importance. We should ask whether, in themselves, these other facts matter.

Therefore

(3) Personal identity cannot be rationally or morally important. What matters can only be one or more of the other facts in which personal identity consists.

Mark Johnston rejects this argument.[1] He calls it an *Argument from Below*, since it claims that, if one fact justs consists in certain others, it can only be these other lower level facts which matter. Johnston replies with what he calls an *Argument from Above*. On his view, even if the lower-level facts do not in themselves matter, the higher-level fact may matter. If it does, the lower-level facts will have a derived significance. They will matter, not in themselves, but because they constitute the higher-level fact.

To illustrate this disagreement, we can start with a different case. Suppose we ask what we want to happen if, through

[1] In his 'Human Concerns Without Superlative Selves', in Dancy (forthcoming).

brain damage, we become irreversibly unconscious. If we were in this state, we would still be alive. But this fact should be understood in a Reductionist way. It may not be the same as the fact that our hearts would still be beating, and our other organs would still be functioning. But it would not be an independent or separately obtaining fact. Our being still alive, though irreversibly unconscious, would just consist in these other facts.

On my Argument from Below, we should ask whether those other facts in themselves matter. If we were irreversibly unconscious, would it be either good for us, or good for others, that our hearts and other organs would still be functioning? If we answer No, we should conclude that it would not matter that we were still alive.

If Johnston were right, we could reject this argument. And we could appeal to an Argument from Above. We might say:

It may not be in itself good that our hearts and other organs would still be functioning. But it is good to be alive. Since that is so, it is rational to hope that, even if we could never regain consciousness, our hearts would go on beating for as long as possible. That would be good because it would constitute our staying alive.

I believe that, of these arguments, mine is more plausible.

Consider next the moral question that such cases raise. Some people ask, in their living wills, that if brain damage makes them irreversibly unconscious, their hearts should be stopped. I believe that we should do what these people ask. But many take a different view. They could appeal to an Argument from Above. They might say:

Even if such people can never regain consciousness, while their hearts are still beating, they can be truly called alive. Since that is so, stopping their hearts would be an act of killing. And, except in self-defence, it is always wrong to kill.

On this view, we should leave these people's hearts to go on beating, for months or even years.

As an answer to the moral question, this seems to me misguided. (It is a separate question what the law should be.)

But, for many people, the word 'kill' has such force that it seems significant whether it applies.

Turn now to a different subject. Suppose that, after trying to decide when people have free will, we become convinced by either of two compatibilist views. On one view, we call choices 'unfree' if they are caused in certain ways, and we call them 'free' if they are caused in certain other ways. On the other view, we call choices 'unfree' if we know how they were caused, and we call them 'free' if we have not yet discovered this.

Suppose next that, when we consider these two grounds for drawing this distinction, we believe that neither, in itself, has the kind of significance that could support making or denying claims about guilt, or desert. There seems to us no such significance in the difference between these kinds of causal determination; and we believe that it cannot matter whether a decision's causes have already been discovered. (Note that, in comparing the Arguments from Above and Below, we need not actually accept these claims. We are asking whether, *if* we accepted the relevant premises, we ought to be persuaded by these arguments.)

On my Argument from Below, if the fact that a choice is free just consists in one of those other facts, and we believe that those other facts cannot in themselves be morally important, we should conclude that it cannot be important whether some person's choice was free. Either choices that are unfree can deserve to be punished, or choices that are free cannot. On a Johnstonian Argument from Above, even if those other facts are not in themselves important—even if, in themselves, they are trivial—they can have a derived importance if and because they constitute the fact that some person's choice was free. As before, the Argument from Below seems to me more plausible.

We can now consider the underlying question on which this disagreement turns.

As I have claimed, if one fact just consists in certain others, the first fact is not an independent or separately obtaining fact. And, in the cases with which we are concerned, it is also, in relation to these other facts, merely a conceptual fact. Thus, if someone is irreversibly unconscious, but his heart is still beating, it is a conceptual fact that this person is still alive. When I call this fact conceptual, I don't mean that it is a fact about our concepts. That this person is alive is a fact about this person. But, if we have already claimed that this person's heart is still beating, when we claim that he is still alive, we do not give further information about reality. We only give further information about our use of the words 'person' and 'alive'.

When we turn to ask what matters, the central question is this. Suppose we agree that it does not matter, in itself, that such a person's heart is still beating. Could we claim that, in another way, this fact does matter, because it makes it correct to say that this person is still alive? If we answer Yes, we are treating language as more important than reality. We are claiming that, even if some fact does not in itself matter, it may matter if and because it allows a certain word to be applied.

This, I believe, is irrational. On my view, what matters are the facts about the world, given which some concept applies. If the facts about the world have no rational or moral significance, and the fact that the concept applies is not a further difference in what happens, this conceptual fact cannot be significant.

Johnston brings a second charge against my argument. If physicalism were true, he claims, all facts would just consist in facts about fundamental particles. Considered in themselves, these facts about particles would have no rational or moral importance. If we apply an Argument from Below, we must conclude that nothing has any importance. He remarks: 'this is not a proof of Nihilism. It is a reductio ad absurdum.'

Given what I have suggested here, this charge can, I think, be answered. There may perhaps be a sense in which, if physicalism were true, all facts would just consist in facts about fundamental particles. But that is not the kind of reduction which I had in mind. When I claim that personal identity just consists in certain other facts, I have in mind a closer and partly conceptual relation. Claims about personal identity may not mean the same as claims about physical and/or psychological continuity. But, if we knew the facts about these continuities, and understood the concept of a person, we would thereby know, or would be able to work out, the facts about persons. Hence my claim that, if we know the other facts, questions about personal identity should be taken to be questions, not about reality, but only about our language. These claims do not apply to facts about fundamental particles. It is not true for example that, if we knew how the particles moved in some person's body, and understood our concepts, we would thereby know, or be able to work out, all of the relevant facts about this person. To understand the world around us, we need more than physics and a knowledge of our own language.

My argument does not claim that, whenever there are facts at different levels, it is always the lowest-level facts which matter. That is clearly false. We are discussing cases where, relative to the facts at some lower level, the higher-level fact is, in the sense that I have sketched, merely conceptual. My claim is that such conceptual facts cannot be rationally or morally important. What matters is reality, not how it is described. So this view might be called *realism about importance*.

If we are Reductionists about persons, and Realists about importance, we should conclude that personal identity is not what matters. Can we accept that conclusion?

Most of us believe that we should care about our future because it will be *our* future. I believe that what matters is not identity but certain other relations. To help us to decide between these views, we should consider cases where identity and those relations do not coincide.

Which these cases are depends on which criterion of identity we accept. I shall start with the simplest form of the

Physical Criterion, according to which a person continues to exist if and only if that person's body continues to exist. That must be the view of those who believe that persons just are bodies. And it is the view of several of the people who identify persons with human beings. Let's call this the *Bodily Criterion*.

Suppose that, because of damage to my spine, I have become partly paralysed. I have a brother, who is dying of a brain disease. With the aid of new techniques, when my brother's brain ceases to function, my head could be grafted onto the rest of my brother's body. Since we are identical twins, my brain would then control a body that is just like mine, except that it would not be paralysed.

Should I accept this operation? Of those who assume that identity is what matters, three groups would answer No. Some accept the Bodily Criterion. These people believe that, if this operation were performed, I would die. The person with my head tomorrow would be my brother, who would mistakenly think that he was me. Other people are uncertain what would happen. They believe that it would be risky to accept this operation, since the resulting person might not be me. Others give a different reason why I should reject this operation: that it would be indeterminate whether that person would be me. On all these views, it matters who that person would be.

On my view, that question is unimportant. If this operation were performed, the person with my head tomorrow would not only believe that he was me, seem to remember living my life, and be in every other way psychologically like me. These facts would also have their normal cause, the continued existence of my brain. And this person's body would be just like mine. For all these reasons, his life would be just like the life that I would have lived, if my paralysis had been cured. I believe that, given these facts, I should accept this operation. It is irrelevant whether this person would be me.

That may seem all important. After all, if he would not be me, I shall have ceased to exist. But, if that person would not be me, this fact would just consist in another fact. It would just consist in the fact that my body will have been replaced below the neck. When considered on its own, is that second fact important? Can it matter in itself that the blood that will keep my brain alive will circulate, not through my own heart and lungs, but through my brother's heart and lungs? Can it matter in itself that my brain will control, not the rest of my body, but the rest of another body that is exactly similar?

If we believe that these facts would amount to my non-existence, it may be hard to focus on the question whether, in themselves, these facts matter. To make that easier, we should imagine that we accept a different view. Suppose we are convinced that the person with my head tomorrow *would* be me. Would we then believe that it would matter greatly that my head would have been grafted onto this other body? We would not. We would regard my receiving a new torso, and new limbs, as like any lesser transplant, such as receiving a new heart, or new kidneys. As this shows, if it would matter greatly that what will be replaced is not just a few such organs, but my whole body below the neck, that could only be because, if that happened, the resulting person would *not* be me.

According to my argument, we should now conclude that neither of these facts could matter greatly. Since it would not be in itself important that my head would be grafted onto this body, and that would be all there was to the fact that the resulting person would not be me, it would not be in itself important that this person would not be me. Perhaps it would not be irrational to regret these facts a little. But, I believe, they would be heavily outweighed by the fact that, unlike me, the resulting person would not be paralysed.

When it is applied to our own existence, my argument is hard to accept. But, as before, the fundamental question is the relative importance of language and reality.

On my view, what matters is what is going to happen. If I knew that my head could be grafted onto the rest of a body that is just like mine, and that the resulting person would be just like me, I would know enough to decide whether to accept this operation. I need not ask whether the resulting person could be correctly called me. That is not a further difference in what is going to happen.

That may seem a false distinction. What matters, we might say, is whether the resulting person would *be* me. But that person would be me if and only if he could be correctly called me. So, in asking what he could be called, we are not merely asking a conceptual question. We *are* asking about reality.

This objection fails to distinguish two kinds of case. Suppose that I ask my doctor whether, while I receive some treatment, I shall be in pain. That is a factual question. I am asking what will happen. Since pain can be called 'pain', I *could* ask my question in a different way. I could say, 'While I am being treated, will it be correct to describe me as in pain?' But that would be misleading. It would suggest that I am asking how we use the word 'pain'.

In a different case, I might ask that conceptual question. Suppose I know that, while I am crossing the Channel, I shall be feeling sea-sick, as I always do. I might wonder whether that sensation could be correctly called 'pain'. Here too, I could ask my question in a different way. I could say, 'While I am crossing the Channel, shall I be in pain?' But that would be misleading, since it would suggest that I am asking what will happen.

In the medical case, I don't know what conscious state I shall be in. There are different possibilities. In the Channel crossing case, there aren't different possibilities. I already know what state I shall be in. I am merely asking whether that state could be redescribed in a certain way.

It matters whether, while receiving the medical treatment, I shall be in pain. And it matters whether, while crossing the Channel, I shall be sea-sick. But it does not matter whether, in feeling sea-sick, I can be said to be in pain.

Return now to our main example. Suppose I know that my head will be successfully grafted onto my brother's headless body. I ask whether the resulting person will be me. Is this like the medical case, or the case of crossing the Channel? Am I asking what will happen, or whether what I know will happen could be described in a certain way?

On my view, I should take myself to be asking the second. I already know what is going to happen. There will be someone with my head and my brother's body. It is a merely verbal question whether that person will be me. And that is why, even if he won't be me, that doesn't matter.

It may now be objected: 'By choosing this example, you are cheating. Of course you should accept this operation. But that is because the resulting person *would* be you. We should reject the Bodily Criterion. So this case cannot show that identity is not what matters.'

Since there are people who accept this criterion, I am not cheating. It is worth trying to show these people that identity is not what matters. But I accept part of this objection. I agree that we should reject the Bodily Criterion.

Of those who appeal to this criterion, some believe that persons just are bodies. But, if we hold this kind of view, it would be better to identify a person with that person's brain, or nervous system. Consider next those who believe that persons are animals of a certain kind, viz. human beings. We could take this view, but reject the Bodily Criterion. We could claim that animals continue to exist if there continue to exist, and to function, the most important parts of their bodies. And we could claim that, at least in the case of human beings, the brain is so important that its survival counts as the survival of this human being. On both these views, in my imagined case, the person with my head tomorrow would be me. And that is what, on reflection, most of us would believe.

My own view is similar. I would state this view, not as a claim about reality, but as a conceptual claim. On my view, it would not be incorrect to call this person me; and this would be the best description of this case.

If we agree that this person would be me, I would still argue that this fact is not what matters. What is important is not identity, but one or more of the other facts in which identity consists. But I concede that, when identity coincides with these other facts, it is harder to decide whether we accept that argument's conclusion. So, if we reject the Bodily Criterion, we must consider other cases.

Suppose that we accept the Brain-Based version of the Psychological Criterion. On this view, if there will be one future person who is psychologically continuous with me, because he will have enough of my brain, that person will be me. But psychological continuity without its normal cause, the continued existence of enough of my brain, does not suffice for identity. My Replica would not be me.

Remember next that an object can continue to exist even if all its components are gradually replaced. Suppose that, every time some wooden ship comes into port, a few of its planks are replaced. Before long, the same ship may be entirely composed of different planks.

Assume, once again, that I need surgery. All of my brain cells have a defect which, in time, would be fatal. Surgeons could replace all these cells, inserting new cells that are exact replicas, except that they have no defect.

The surgeons could proceed in either of two ways. In *Case One*, there would be a hundred operations. In each operation, the surgeons would remove a hundredth part of my brain, and insert replicas of those parts. In *Case Two*, the surgeons would first remove all the existing parts of my brain and then insert all of their replicas.

There is a real difference here. In Case One, my brain would continue to exist, like a ship with all of its planks gradually replaced. In Case Two, my brain would cease to exist, and my body would be given a new brain.

This difference, though, is much smaller than that between ordinary survival and teletransportation. In both cases, there will later be a person whose brain will be just like my present brain, but without the defects, and who will therefore be psychologically continuous with me. And, in *both* cases, this person's brain will be made of the very same new cells, each of which is a replica of one of my existing cells. The difference between the cases is merely the way in which these new cells are inserted. In Case One, the surgeons alternate between removing and inserting. In Case Two, they do all the removing before all the inserting.

On the Brain-Based Criterion, this is the difference between life and death. In Case One, the resulting person would be me. In Case Two he would *not* be me, so I would cease to exist.

Can this difference matter? Reapply the Argument from Below. This difference consists in the fact that, rather than alternating between removals and insertions, the surgeon does all the removing before all the inserting. Considered on its own, can this matter? I believe not. We would not think it mattered if it did not constitute the fact that the resulting person would not be me. But if this fact does not in itself matter, and that is all there is to the fact that in Case Two I would cease to exist, I should conclude that my ceasing to exist does not matter.

Suppose next that you regard these as problem cases, ones where you do not know what would happen to me. Return to the simpler Physical Spectrum. In each of the cases in this range, some proportion of my cells will be replaced with exact duplicates. With some proportions—20 per cent, say, or 50, or 70—most of us would be uncertain whether the resulting person would be me. (As before, if we do not believe that here, my remarks could be transferred, with adjustments, to the Combined Spectrum.)

On my view, in all of the cases in this range, it is a merely conceptual question whether the resulting person would be me. Even without answering this question, I can know just what is going to happen. If there is anything that I don't know, that is merely a fact about how we could describe what is going to happen. And that conceptual question is not even, I believe, interesting. It is merely verbal, like the question whether, if I replaced some of its parts, I would still have the same audio system.

When we imagine these cases from a first-person point of view, it may still be hard to believe that this is merely a verbal question. If I don't know whether, tomorrow, I shall still exist, it may be hard to believe that I know what is going to happen. But what is it that I don't know? If there are different possibilities, at the level of what happens, what is the difference between them? In what would that difference consist? If I had a soul, or Cartesian Ego, there might be different possibilities. Perhaps, even if *n* per cent of my cells were replaced, my soul would keep its intimate relation with my brain. Or perhaps another soul would take over. But, we have assumed, there are no such entities. What else could the difference be? When the resulting person wakes up tomorrow, what could make it either true, or false, that he is me?

It may be said that, in asking what will happen, I am asking what I can expect. Can I expect to wake up again? If that person will be in pain, can I expect to feel that pain? But this does not help. These are just other ways of asking whether that person will or will not be me. In appealing to what I can expect, we do not explain what would make these different possibilities.

We may believe that this difference needs no explanation. It may seem enough to say: Perhaps that person will be me, and perhaps he won't. Perhaps I shall exist tomorrow, and perhaps I shan't. It may seem that these must be different possibilities.

That, however, is an illusion. If I shall still exist tomorrow, that fact must consist in certain others. For there to be two possibilities, so that it might be either true or false that I shall exist tomorrow, there must be some other difference between these possibilities. There would be such a difference, for example, if, between now and tomorrow, my brain and body might either remain unharmed, or be blown to pieces. But, in our imagined case, there is no such other difference. I already know that there will be someone whose brain and body will consist partly of these cells, and partly of new cells, and that this person will be psychologically like me. There aren't, at the level of what happens, different possible outcomes. There is no further essence of me, or property of me-ness, which either might or might not be there.

If we turn to the conceptual level, there *are* different possibilities. Perhaps that future person could be correctly called me. Perhaps he could be correctly called someone else. Or perhaps neither would be correct. That, however, is the only way in which it could be either true, or false, that this person would be me.

The illusion may persist. Even when I know the other facts, I may want reality to go in one of two ways. I may want it to be true that I shall still exist tomorrow. But all that could be true is that we use language in one of two ways. Can it be rational to care about that?

III

I am now assuming that we accept the Brain-Based Psychological Criterion. We believe that, if there will be one future person who will have enough of my brain to be psychologically continuous with me, that person would be me. On this view, there is another way to argue that identity is not what matters.

We can first note that, just as I could survive with less than my whole body, I could survive with less than my whole brain. People have survived, and with little psychological change, even when, through a stroke or injury, they have lost the use of half their brain.

Let us next suppose that the two halves of my brain could each fully support ordinary psychological functioning. That may in fact be true of certain people. If it is not, we can suppose that, through some technological advance, it has been made true of me. Since our aim is to test our beliefs about what matters, there is no harm in making such assumptions.

We can now compare two more possible operations. In the first, after half my brain is destroyed, the other half would be successfully transplanted into the empty skull of a body that is just like mine. Given our assumptions, we should conclude that, here too, I would survive. Since I would survive if my brain were transplanted, and I would survive with only half my brain, it would be unreasonable to deny that I would survive if that remaining half were transplanted. So, in this *Single Case*, the resulting person would be me.

Consider next the *Double Case*, or *My Division*. Both halves of my brain would be successfully transplanted, into different bodies that are just like mine. Two people would wake up, each of whom has half my brain, and is, both physically and psychologically, just like me.

Since these would be two different people, it cannot be true that each of them is me. That would be a contradiction. If each of them was me, each would be one and the same person: me. So they could not be two different people.

Could it be true that only one of them is me? That is not a contradiction. But, since I have the same relation to each of these people, there is nothing that could make me one of them rather than the other. It cannot be true, of either of these people, that he is the one who could be correctly called me.

How should I regard these two operations? Would they preserve what matters in survival? In the Single Case, the one resulting person would be me. The relation between me now and that future person is just an instance of the relation between me now and myself tomorrow. So that relation would contain what matters. In the Double Case, my relation to that person would be just the same. So this relation must still contain what matters. Nothing is missing. But that person cannot here be claimed to be me. So identity cannot be what matters.

We may object that, if that person isn't me, something *is* missing. *I'm* missing. That may seem to make all the difference. How can everything still be there if *I'm* not there?

Everything is still there. The fact that I'm not there is not a real absence. The relation between me now and that future person is in itself the same. As in the Single Case, he has half my brain, and he is just like me. The difference is only that, in this Double Case, I also have the same relation to the other resulting person. Why am I not there? The explanation is only this. When this relation holds between me now and a single person in the future, we can be called one and the same person. When this relation holds between me now and *two* future people, I cannot be called one and the same as each of these people. But that is not a difference in the nature or the content of this relation. In the Single Case, where half my brain will be successfully transplanted, my prospect is survival. That prospect contains what matters. In the Double Case, where both halves will be successfully transplanted, nothing would be lost.

It can be hard to believe that identity is not what matters. But that is easier to accept when we see why, in this example, it is true. It may help to consider this analogy. Imagine a community of persons who are like us, but with two exceptions. First, because of facts about their reproductive system, each couple has only two children, who are always twins. Second, because of special features of their psychology, it is of great importance for the development of each child that it should not, through the death of its sibling, become an only child. Such children suffer psychological damage. It is thus believed, in this community, that it matters greatly that each child should have a twin.

Now suppose that, because of some biological change, some of the children in this community start to be born as triplets. Should their parents think this a disaster, because these children don't have twins? Clearly not. These children don't have twins only because they each have *two* siblings. Since each child has two siblings, the trio must be called, not twins, but triplets. But none of them will suffer damage as an only child. These people should revise their view. What matters isn't having a twin: it is having at least one sibling.

In the same way, we should revise our view about identity over time. What matters isn't that there will be someone alive who will be me. It is rather that there will be at least one living person who will be psychologically continuous with me as I am now, and/or who has enough of my brain. When there will be only one such person, he can be described as me. When there will be two such people, we cannot claim that each will be me. But that is as trivial as the fact that, if I had two identical siblings, they could not be called my twins.[2]

IV

If, as I have argued, personal identity is not what matters, we must ask what does matter. There are several possible answers. And, depending on our answer, there are several further implications. Thus there are several moral questions which I have no time even to mention. I shall end with another remark about our concern for our own future.

That concern is of several kinds. We may want to survive partly so that our hopes and ambitions will be achieved. We may also care about our future in the kind of way in which we care about the well-being of certain other people, such as our relatives or friends. But most of us have, in addition, a distinctive kind of egoistic concern. If I know that my child will be in pain, I may care about his pain more than I would about my own future pain. But I cannot fearfully anticipate my child's pain. And if I knew that my Replica would take up my life where I leave off, I would not look forward to that life.

---

[2] In many contexts, we need to distinguish two senses of 'what matters in survival'. What matters in the *prudential* sense is what gives us reason for special concern about our future. What matters in the *desirability* sense is what makes our survival good. But, in the examples I have been discussing, these two coincide. On my view, even if we won't survive, we could have what matters *in* survival. If there will be at least one living person who will both be psychological continuous with me, and have enough of my brain, my relation to that person contains what matters in the prudential sense. So it also preserves what matters in the desirability sense. It is irrelevant whether that person will be me.

The unimportance of identity

This kind of concern may, I believe, be weakened, and be seen to have no ground, if we come to accept a Reductionist view. In our thoughts about our own identity, we are prone to illusions. That is why the so-called 'problem cases' seem to raise problems: why we find it hard to believe that, when we know the other facts, it is an empty or a merely verbal question whether we shall still exist. Even after we accept a Reductionist view, we may continue, at some level, to think and feel as if that view were not true. Our own continued existence may still seem an independent fact, of a peculiarly deep and simple kind. And that belief may underlie our anticipatory concern about our own future.

There are, I suspect, several causes of that illusory belief. I have discussed one cause here: our conceptual scheme. Though we need concepts to think about reality, we sometimes confuse the two. We mistake conceptual facts for facts about reality. And, in the case of certain concepts, those that are most loaded with emotional or moral significance, we can be led seriously astray. Of these loaded concepts, that of our own identity is, perhaps, the most misleading.

Even the use of the word 'I' can lead us astray. Consider the fact that, in a few years, I shall be dead. This fact can seem depressing. But the reality is only this. After a certain time, none of the thoughts and experiences that occur will be directly causally related to this brain, or be connected in certain ways to these present experiences. That is all this fact involves. And, in that redescription, my death seems to disappear.

3

An Experimentalist Looks at Identity

HENRY HARRIS

I like to think that it is common ground between philosophers and scientists that no two material objects can be qualitatively identical in the universe as it now is. This view stems, in the first instance, from the common experience that objects that initially seem to be the same always turn out to be distinguishable on closer examination or on examination by more refined techniques; but, for scientists, it is strongly reinforced by Heisenberg's demonstration that the fundamental particles of which all matter is composed cannot in principle be delimited singly. We are now resigned to the fact that we shall never know whether, for example, one particular electron is qualitatively identical to any other. Our concept of the electron is governed by equations that are derived from the stochastic behaviour of large populations of such particles. These are statistical statements and are bound to remain so. In the world of common experience, it is a trivial matter to show that no two objects are qualitatively identical; in the world of subatomic particles, whether two individual particles of the same kind are qualitatively identical is an unanswerable and perhaps meaningless question. If, then, to use conventional terminology, the proposition x is identical to y can be shown to be true, then x and y cannot be two material objects in the existing universe. So what can x and y be?

They may simply be elements in an agreed formalism, for example, $2 + 2 = 3 + 1$. This is not, of course, a statement of material or physical identity; it simply asserts equivalence within the system. It is a symbolic example of Leibniz's famous theorem which, translated into a modern idiom, states that if, of two things, one can be substituted for the other, then they are the same. $x = y$ in a formal system simply means that anywhere you see x you can substitute y and the outcome will not be changed. Experimentalists have no problem with substitutivity in formal systems, but their main interest in such systems lies in their ability to illuminate the structure of the material world. Experimentalists wish to know not only whether x can be substituted for y in a formal system; they also wish to know whether it is true that whatever stands for x in the material world is the same thing as whatever stands for y. As Gödel has shown, truth for any formal system cannot be defined within the system itself. If we wish to know whether formal equivalence does in fact correspond to identity in the real world, then we shall be obliged at some point to leave the confines of the formal system and confront that world, where, among other things, we can expect to find that two shillings and two shillings are indeed equivalent to three shillings and one shilling, but that when it comes to raindrops, two and two are not at all equivalent to three and one.

We are agreed then that in the real world the question of qualitative identity does not arise in connection with two separable material objects. It arises only when we are unsure whether two phenomena observed independently, either in space or time, represent two different things or simply two different views of the one thing. We know, without even bothering to examine the matter, that no two peas are identical, however alike they may be; but it took centuries of astronomical observation to decide whether, to use Frege's example, the morning star and the evening star were one and the same thing. Questions of identity in the material world are always empirical questions, and they can be decided only by empirical methods. Feigl (1953) allows that this is true when x and y are things (what I have been calling material objects), but argues that the 'identity of concepts' may also be decided by deduction. But the example he gives to illustrate identity of concepts is once again simply a case of substitution or equivalence within a formal system: $2^3 = \sqrt{64}$. I have already mentioned the limitations that Gödel's theorem places on the power of arithmetical systems, but even within such systems, what passes for a deduction is often hard to distinguish from empirical enquiry. For all but the most elementary exercises, (and even these would not be elementary for an untutored child) exploration of the ramifications of an arithmetical system may be difficult, fraught with error or uncertainty, frustrated by impasses that require the development of new methods, subject to correction or rejection by subsequent investigators. Since empirical enquiry certainly does not exclude deduction, it is not easy to discern a fundamental difference between a serious arithmetical investigation and what is conventionally called an empirical enquiry other than that the investigator operates with symbols on the one hand and material objects on the other.

But there is a deeper question. Philosophers commonly make a distinction between a relationship that is contingent and one that is necessary. I am not sure that this distinction is as fundamental as it appears. If it is agreed that all questions of identity in the material world are empirical questions, then the identity relationship between any two phenomena in that world is, in this terminology, contingent. 'Necessary' identity is a relationship that exists only in formal systems, whether mathematical or logical, and is simply a reflection of the rules of the formalism. We say that x is 'necessarily' identical to y only because we have been drilled for centuries to reason within a framework of Aristotelian syllogisms that impose such (to my mind essentially tautological) relationships. Let me illustrate this point by examining an argument that we owe to Kripke (1979). It concerns the identity or non-identity of mind and brain; and although few will now find the case that Kripke makes convincing, the structure of the argument and the nature of the conclusion drawn from it remain of interest. Kripke's thesis may be summarized as follows. If x is identical to y, then any property that x has, y must also have. x is, however, surely identical to x, and necessarily so. In other words, x has the property of being *necessarily* identical to x. But if x is identical to y, then, by substitution, y also must have the property of being necessarily identical to x. Hence, if y is identical to x, it is necessarily identical to x. Kripke then applies this formal reasoning to the relationship between mind and brain. If mind and brain are identical, he argues, then they also must be necessarily identical. But it is obvious that mind and brain are not necessarily identical. If identical at all, they can only be contingently so. It therefore follows, according to Kripke, that mind and brain are not identical.

Experimentalists who consider themselves to be working on the mind or on the brain find this argument laughable; but this is not due to any error in the formalism. So long as Kripke stays within his formal system, the substitution of properties that he makes is unimpeachable. But when he substitutes elements of the real world (minds and brains) for x and y, the argument breaks down completely. For whereas it is true that my brain necessarily is my brain and nothing else, it is also true that my brain can only be contingently identical with my mind. And there is no paradox, even if it should turn out in the end that mind and brain are the same thing. What we have here is simply an example of an incompatibility with which every experimentalist is intimately familiar: the failure of a formal model to accommodate the complexities of reality. In formal systems identity means no more than substitutivity within the system; but in the world of sticks and stones additional or other criteria apply.

However, what disturbs the experimental scientist more deeply than the inapplicability of Kripke's logic to the real world is the illusion that a question as complex and as intractable as the relationship between mind and brain could be disposed of by an exercise in formal logic. It is startling how innocent some of the arguments are that have been deployed to dismiss the possibility that mind and brain are identical. Shaffer (1970), for example, argues that it makes no sense to say that the mind is either inside the head or outside it; but since the brain clearly is inside the head, mind and brain cannot be identical. Similarly, Nagel (1970) argues that it makes no sense to say that the thought or pain that I had when I was in my office was itself in the office; but my brain obviously was, so mind processes and brain processes cannot be identical. Kenny (1989) presents two arguments. 'First, there can be brains without minds: a human brain that has spent all its life in a vat cannot have thoughts and therefore does not have a mind, no matter how similar it may be electrically and neurologically to a normal human brain. Secondly, it is conceivable that there should be minds without brains. If, when I die, it turns out that there is nothing but sawdust in my skull, that would be an astonishing miracle. But if it happened it would not cast the slightest doubt on the fact that I have a mind, which is proved beyond question by the fact that I know English and am using it to write this book.' Any number of philosophers have argued that mind and brain cannot be identical because the words we use to describe states of mind—pain, desire, guilt, pride—are inapplicable to the brain.

Can such arguments really provide a genuine solution to so great a problem? It is indeed a little odd to talk of the mind being inside the head or in an office. Nonetheless, if something goes wrong with my mind, for example if I start hallucinating, no psychiatrist can do much about it if I refuse to take my mind along to his consulting room. What would a brain that had spent the whole of its life in a vat really be like? Even if the vat were unbelievably ingenious and able to provide all the metabolic requirements of a developing brain, nothing like an adult brain would emerge. For the development of a normal brain requires a continuous stream of appropriate and accurately timed sensory inputs. If, for example, an eye is deprived of vision at a critical stage in the elaboration of the visual pathways, then those parts of the brain that subserve that eye will fail to develop normally and will remain permanently defective. The structures that house memory will not be formed unless the brain is given something to memorize. The best we could hope for from such a vat would be an inchoate mass of surviving brain tissue that would certainly not have anything like normal electrical circuitry or normal neurological function. What would it prove, if such a structure failed to acquire properties that we would agree to call mind? And how, in the absence of speech, movement, or any other form of communication would we know whether it had acquired them? It would indeed be a miracle if, after his death, Anthony Kenny's head were found to be full of sawdust. But the miracle would not be that he was able to write an interesting book on the metaphysics of mind despite the fact that he had no brain. For we know that when he wrote that book, he walked and talked and ate and slept, all of which would have been impossible if he had had no brain. The miracle would be that such a good brain was so rapidly transformed to sawdust after his death; and that miracle, regrettably, sheds no light on the relationship between mind and brain.

All these arguments suffer from two major defects. The first is the tendentious nature of the language that we use to describe states of mind. This language evolved long before we knew anything about the biological function of the brain. Aristotle considered the heart to be the seat of intelligence and attached no great importance to the brain, regarding it merely as a cooling device to prevent the heart from becoming overheated. Since Aristotle's ideas dominated European intellectual life for two millenia, it is not surprising that the language that we use to describe states of mind still contains words like heart-rending, bilious, or splenetic. Before the second half of the nineteenth century, when some glimmer of the complexity and power of the brain began to dawn on the European consciousness, it would have been entirely implausible to apply to the brain the vocabulary used in common speech to describe the activities of the mind. But this incongruence had its origins not only in misplaced notions of where in the body the seat of intelligence might be. An equally important influence was the doctrine, almost universally accepted until quite modern times, that, after death, the mind left the body and continued to exist as a soul. This, together with the attendant vocabulary, made it difficult to allow that the mind could be precisely localized to any particular site in the body. Arguments against the identity of mind and brain based on the fact that certain terms commonly used in connection with the mind are inapplicable to the brain, and vice versa, are distant echoes of the doctrine of disembodiment. It is not easy to accept that if I had a thought in my office, then that was where the thought was, and that if I had a pain while I was in bed, then that was where the pain was.

The second defect is the highly simplified and mechanistic view of the brain that many of these arguments reveal. Some writers seem to regard the brain as no more than a collection of cells communicating with each other by electric currents, an object that one really could imagine developing in a vat or being wired up to do this or that much like a telephone exchange. The application of electrophysiological methods made possible by the invention of the thermionic valve did indeed produce a torrent of new information about the nervous system, but no electrophysiologist now supposes that the currents he records are anything other than indicators of more profound biological events. We know, for example, that stimulation of specific regions within the brain can produce acute pleasure or acute pain. We know that memory, both long and short term, is stored there, and although we do not know what form it is stored in, we do know pretty accurately where that store is. We know that if the appropriate loci are stimulated, visual, auditory, or olfactory hallucinations can be produced which reflect genuine experiences. We know that by administering drugs that act on the brain, we can modify mood, elate, sedate, induce sleep or loss of consciousness altogether. We know that simple chemical errors in small pieces of DNA can result in specific mental defects. None of this proves that mind and brain are identical, but the case must be taken more seriously than it often has been. It does not help to sell the brain short.

Clearly, the central problem is the classical one of deciding whether two sets of correlated observations represent different aspects of the one event or whether there are two linked or causally related events. Place (1970), discussing this question in the context of mind and brain, insists that there must be some logical criteria that would permit us to decide it. Must there? As I have said, the identity or non-identity of material objects observed under different circumstances is an empirical question that can be decided only by empirical methods; and while these may include the operations of formal logic, they cannot be replaced by them. No experimentalist believes that a satisfactory explanation of the relationship between mind and brain is imminent. One need only reflect on the length of time it took to provide a satisfactory explanation of how a flame could be produced by the chemical conjunction of carbon and oxygen. Nor is it to be expected that the identity of mind and brain will be established or disproved at one blow by some *experimentum crucis*. But it is probable that increasingly refined investigations of the brain will gradually lead us to abandon dualistic concepts, because they will have become unnecessary and unhelpful; or, less probably, these same investigations will lead us to accept two separate entities because new phenomena will have been discovered that cannot be explained otherwise.

Theories of mind bear directly on the question of personal identity. Here, the meaning of the word 'identity' is more difficult to put one's finger on and is related only tenuously to the ways in which I have used this word so far. Personal identity encompasses the idea of self-consciousness, personality, character and, after Locke, usually presupposes the existence of memory. There is an entertaining literature devoted to the discussion of just which human characteristics are indispensable or quintessential for the maintenance of personal identity. Let us steer clear of this discussion, because, as Quine says (1987), it all boils down in the end to what one chooses to call a person. But there is one aspect of this literature that demands comment here because it deploys anatomical and physiological data that appear to lend greater weight to certain arguments than they deserve. I refer to those speculative exercises in which brains are transplanted from one individual to another, accurately replicated and transported to other worlds, divided into two equipotent halves, and so on—anatomical exercises in philosophy. Wiggins (1967) seems to have been the originator of the genre, but Parfit (1986) is our undisputed contemporary master.

To begin with, let us distinguish between a thought experiment and a flight of fancy. A thought experiment is an empirical investigation that one does in one's head. One explores a hypothesis or the content of a proposition by testing it out against the constraints imposed by the image one has of the relevant parts of the real world. This is not, of course, as good as trying it out against the constraints imposed by the real world itself, because one's images of the world are inevitably incomplete and in varying degrees faulty. But in doing a thought experiment, one's aim is essentially the same as when one does a genuine experiment. What one seeks to establish is whether the hypothesis or the proposition is plausible, how far it will go when tested against reality in the one case, or against one's conception of reality in the other. A flight of fancy is something else altogether. Here one can propose situations and conclusions that are completely unrestrained by one's vision of reality, that one knows to be implausible. One does not explore a flight of fancy in order to test the plausibility of an empirical proposition. One follows it through in its own right in order to see where it will lead. This has its interest, but one is always left wondering at the end about the relevance that the conclusions drawn from flights of fancy might have to what one finds in the real world.

In his effort to provide a new philosophical basis for moral behaviour, Parfit seeks to extend the concept of personal identity. He does this by exploring the consequences of a series of imaginary operations in which the brain is replicated and the replica transplanted to a new body, or is divided into two identical, fully functional halves which are then similarly transplanted. Doubtless he would deny that these para-anatomical exercises are flights of fancy in my sense. He would argue, in fact he has argued, that they are perfectly reasonable extensions of empirical observations that *have* been made in the real world. Indeed, he repeatedly insists that this is so, for he is conscious that the plausibility of what he has to say depends on his conjectures being firmly grounded in reality. Here are three examples from *Reasons and Persons*, of what Parfit writes about the division of the brain into two halves:

It is in fact true that one hemisphere is enough. There are many people who have survived, when a stroke or injury puts out of action one of their hemispheres. With his remaining hemisphere, such a person may need to re-learn certain things, such as adult speech, or how to control both hands. But this is possible.

And it is a fact that people with disconnected hemispheres have two separate streams of consciousness—two series of thoughts and experiences, in having each of which they are unaware of having the other.

The one feature of the case that might be held to be *deeply* impossible—the division of a person's consciousness into two separate streams—is the feature that has actually happened. It would have been important if this had been impossible, since this might have supported some claim about what we really are.

These assertions are highly questionable. They seem to rest on a mistaken view of what actually happens to the brain when one seriously damages it. The *fons et origo* of these para-anatomical conjectures is the work of Sperry, who studied some remarkable cases in which injury or surgery had divided all or most of the nerve fibres that connect the two halves of the cerebral cortex. This work has been made to bear much too heavy a weight of interpretation. Let me make one or two elementary anatomical points about the structure of the brain. The two halves of the brain are not functionally or structurally equivalent. All functions associated with speech and language, including language-based memory, are, in right-handed people, normally located in the left hemisphere, not the right. Injuries to or removal of these regions in the left hemisphere impair or abolish language-based functions, including long-term memory. Corresponding lesions in the right hemisphere do not. Since a highly asymmetrical brain greatly reduces the plausibility of many of Parfit's conjectures, he takes his stand on what he believes to be a group of special cases in which the two halves of the brain are symmetrical: 'Suppose', he writes, 'that I am one of a minority with two exactly similar hemispheres.' I fear that this is a minority of zero. It is indeed true that some 1 per cent of right-handed people do have some representation of speech functions in the right as well as in the left hemisphere, but in no case known to me has it been established that a full panoply of speech functions is equally well represented in both hemispheres. Although there is still some uncertainty about the significance of bilateral representation of speech functions in right-handed people who appear to be normal, present evidence suggests that this is probably a compensatory mechanism that enables the right hemisphere, during the early development of the brain, to take over some functions that are aberrant or damaged in the left hemisphere. In left-handed and ambidextrous people, there is a much higher incidence of speech representation in both hemispheres, and in left-handed and ambidextrous people with known early brain damage, the incidence is higher still. Bilateral representation of speech functions is evidence of the brain attempting to cope as best it can with some abnormality or deficit of function; it is not a gratuitous duplication of function.

Parfit repeatedly stresses that many people have survived after complete removal of one hemisphere. So they have, but they are thereafter severely handicapped. Complete removal of a hemisphere is a drastic procedure that some surgeons undertake to deal with otherwise intractable brain lesions, for example malignant brain tumours or unmanageable epilepsy. (Strokes, by the way, do not completely remove one hemisphere.) Complete removal of a hemisphere results in paralysis of the opposite half of the body and, if it is the left hemisphere that is removed, loss of speech functions and language-based memory. It is not the case that a right-handed individual who has lost his left hemisphere 'may need to re-learn certain things, such as adult speech, or how to control both hands' as Parfit puts it. If it is an adult we are talking about, the remaining hemisphere cannot make good the functions that have been lost: the individual will remain very largely paralysed on one side and he will remain aphasic. In children during the first two or three years of life, when the brain is developing rapidly, some degree of compensation can occur and language function may be acquired by the right hemisphere. But a detailed examination of the extent of this compensation reveals that it invariably falls far short of normal (Vargha-Khadem *et al.* 1985). So, while it is true that an individual with one hemisphere may survive, his condition does not offer much encouragement for the view that, with a little adaptation, one can get along with half a brain as well as one can with a whole one.

Sperry's studies on split brains have had a remarkable effect on popular notions of brain functions, but I do not believe that they contribute anything to the philosophy of mind. The two halves of the brain normally function in concert. To achieve this, a system of fibres exists that connects one half of the cerebral cortex with the other and ensures that information received, processed, and stored in one half is, where necessary for normal function, transmitted to the other. When this system of fibres is interrupted, information deposited in one half of the brain cannot be so transmitted. It is possible to devise tests to show that, in such cases, one half of the brain may completely fail to register information delivered to the other half, so that a different store of information may be deposited into each half. If the system of communication is completely severed, the two halves of the cortex will operate independently. It is difficult to know precisely what is meant by 'two streams of consciousness', but it is certainly not the case that in these split-brain patients the complete panoply of mental functions is duplicated. A more realistic description of the situation is that elements of the 'stream of consciousness' that are normally co-ordinated in the two halves of the brain are now no longer so. The net result is impairment (usually very serious) of cerebral function, not enhancement or *de novo* duplication. Parfit's repeated contention that his para-anatomical exercises are grounded in clinical reality is baseless.

The smallest unit that can encompass a complete personality is a complete brain. Of the para-anatomical exercises that have been proposed, it is therefore perhaps just worth considering, in the light of current knowledge, what the consequences might be of transplanting a whole brain from one person into the body of another, if this could be done. The difficulties are often dismissed as essentially technical, a matter of connecting the donated brain to the nerves of the recipient; but this does rather make light of the problem. To make these connections, many millions of nerve fibres emanating from the brain would need to be accurately joined to the corresponding fibres in the recipient's spinal cord. Moreover, there will certainly be many fibres emanating from any particular brain that will have no corresponding terminals in another's spinal cord; and vice versa. At best, only an incomplete connection will ever be possible. But let us suppose that some form of functional union between the donor's brain and the recipient's decerebrated nervous system can be achieved. What are the consequences likely to be for the donor's personal identity?

Parfit asserts that 'there is no reason to suppose that being transplanted into a very different body would disrupt my psychological continuity'. Quinton (1975) also assumes that the personality of the individual who donates the brain would persist, at least in its essentials, in the new body in which it finds itself. 'It would be odd', he writes, 'for a six-year old girl to display the character of Winston Churchill, odd indeed to the point of outrageousness, but it is not utterly inconceivable. At first, no doubt, the girl's display of dogged endurance, a world-historical comprehensiveness of outlook, and so forth, would strike one as distasteful and pretentious in so young a child. But if she kept it up the impression would wear off.' But surely this is a very unrealistic end-result. At the very least, Winston Churchill's brain would cease to be regulated by a male hormone system and would be subject to the control of a highly immature, but later adolescent and eventually adult, female hormone system. Some defining elements of Churchill's character might well gradually disappear. Would the personality that survived still be recognizable as that of Winston Churchill? Quinton could counter that while the new body might exert some profound influences on the donated brain, they would be influences of a quite general kind and would not have the specificity that characterizes the personality of a particular individual. But that is because Quinton's thought experiment is highly asymmetrical: the personality of the donor is completely specified, whereas that of the recipient is anonymous and not specified beyond the fact that she is a 6-year-old girl. Let us suppose that, instead of being transplanted into the body of an anonymous 6-year-old girl, the brain of Winston Churchill was transplanted into the body of Marilyn Monroe in her prime. Marilyn Monroe was a sex goddess adulated by a large part of the American male population and wooed, apparently with success, by an interesting cross-section of it. The body of Marilyn Monroe, bearing Winston Churchill's brain, might continue to be the epicentre of lavish public and private attention. Might not Marilyn Monroe's body then confer highly specific effects on Winston Churchill's brain, effects that would not be conferred by just any female body?

The specificity that Quinton and others seek to reserve for the brain alone, irrespective of what body it finds itself in, is, in the end, the specificity conferred by personal memory. As long as the new creature has Winston Churchill's memories, for Quinton or Parfit it will remain Winston Churchill whatever body houses those memories. But for how long would the transplanted brain retain Winston Churchill's memories? We do not know enough about memory to be able to answer this question with complete confidence. But there is evidence that indicates that long-term memory is long-term because it is continually being reinforced, either by actual experiences or by experiences that, by association, stimulate us to relive elements of that memory in our imagination. It is an open question whether, and to what extent, the long-term memory taken over in Winston Churchill's transplanted brain would continue to be reinforced in its new Marilyn Monroe-dominated ambience. It is altogether possible that most of Winston Churchill's long-term memory would fade away and would be gradually replaced by a totally different long-term memory. In short, Winston Churchill's personal identity, in so far as it resided in his long-term memory, might simply disappear. The most plausible coutcome of such a transplant would be a chimaeric creature that would soon have neither Winston Churchill's nor Marilyn Monroe's personal identity, but a new identity that might show little resemblance either to that of the donor of the brain or to that of the recipient. On this view, neither brain alone nor body alone can be the vector of a stable personal identity.

So we are left with the problem of continuity. At what point in the inexorable operation of the second law of thermodynamics does personal identity cease to exist, or, to put it less ponderously, when does a person cease to be a person? And when did he (or she) begin to be one? Although these questions, especially the latter, are now at the centre of political agitation and provoke great moral indignation, the answers one gives ultimately depend on what definition one chooses to adopt. As Quine (1987) puts it, these questions hinge not on the nature of identity but on what we choose to count as a person: a matter of taste, convention, upbringing, accepted doctrine, code of practice, or simply what parameters of personality we happen to be interested in. For my taste, memory would be an unattractive criterion. Henry Harris in the late stages of Alzheimer's disease, unable to remember what was said to him a moment before, unable to recognize with confidence close members of his family, unsure of his origins, would still have enough of Henry Harris about him to raise no questions of identity, even if that identity is much reduced. There is, however, one parameter of personal identity that does have exceptional significance, not because it solves any philosophical questions, but because it provides a definitive solution to the problem of identification. Now, whatever characteristics we might choose to adopt for our definition of personal identity, the blueprint for that identity is provided by the genetic constitution that each of us inherits from our two parents. It is this blueprint, carried by every nucleated cell in the body, that determines the framework within which personal identity can develop, sets limits to that development and, above all, endows it with its individuality. It is the most rigid of designators: no one but this particular Henry Harris can have my genetic constitution, in this world or any other. This, of course, we have known for a long time, but it is only in the last few years that chemical techniques for the analysis of DNA have reached a level of precision that enables us to identify, with a negligible probability of error, the genetic constitution of any particular individual. If, now, a sample of my DNA were analysed in this way and the record deposited, then a fragment of bone unearthed 200 years from now in some Oxford cemetery could, so long as it retained a little undegraded DNA, provide future archeologists with a certified, unequivocal blueprint of my personal identity and no one else's. This is a more fundamental, and certainly less slippery, marker than memory or any of the other mental states that have been proposed.

Finally a few words about the attempts that have been made to formulate a new ethical frame of reference by extending personal identity beyond the confines of the individual that embodies it. As we have seen, these imaginative extrapolations have no basis in clinical or physiological fact and therefore carry little conviction for those whose task it is to explore the world as they find it. Besides, altruistic behaviour does not require underpinning by such implausible devices. We already have powerful explanatory models, based not only on evolutionary theory but also on direct observation, that provide ample biological justification for altruism (see e.g. Hughes 1988). Although no biologist would now seek to explain the complexity of moral behaviour in man simply in biological terms, arguments that fly in the face of biological reality are very unlikely to succeed. The subtle interaction of evolutionary necessity and cultural transmission will give us as good an explanation of moral behaviour as we are likely to get.

4

Sexual Identity: Reality or Construction?

MICHAEL RUSE

=====

Well, of course, this is a false dilemma. Because something is real, it does not mean that it cannot be a construct. Nor does its being a construct mean that it cannot be real. The Constitution of the USA is constructed, but it is more real to most Americans than are physical objects—certainly those beyond their borders. But simply settling the question this quickly would be a pity, because, as one moves towards the answer, sexuality raises some interesting problems. So, in a spirit of enquiry, I will pull back and start the discussion at the beginning. And, while I pride myself on not being one of those philosophers who think that all issues collapse into matters of language, it is the case that the topic of sexuality is plagued by confusing and sloppy overlapping terms, so that is a good place to start.

Sex

Whatever else we can say about the concept of 'sex', it is a fact that in humans it comes in two varieties: male and female. In this we are like other mammals and many other members of the living world. But it is by no means a majority position. Most organisms do not have sex. They are 'asexual', meaning that they can reproduce themselves, for sex is to do with reproduction. Organisms which have sex need one of each kind, male and female, to produce more members of their species.

65

In humans, as in other organisms, sex is marked by certain organs which are used for reproduction. One could, I suppose, try to characterize these organs without reference to function, purely anatomically or physiologically. But I am not sure why one would, especially if one takes seriously Darwinian evolutionary theory, believing not only that organisms (humans) are the product of natural processes but that features are characterized by their adaptive utility (Ruse 1982). We have what we have because of the ends that they serve. In humans, males have penises and testicles and so forth, designed to produce sperm and to transfer it into a female's body. In humans, females have vaginas and wombs and breasts and so forth, designed to accept sperm which can fertilize their eggs, to house the developing human (fetus), and to succour it for some period after birth.

Associated with the features directly involved in reproduction are so-called 'secondary' characteristics. These include such facts as that males tend to be bigger and stronger than females, and that (as always talking about humans unless otherwise specified) males have facial hair unlike females, not to mention a tendency to baldness. For what it is worth, although it is no part of my main concern, my suspicion is that biologists today think that some although perhaps not all are under the direct control of selection (Symons 1979). Today, many think them a by-product of other factors, like internal bodily secretions (Gould 1977). Darwin (1871) also thought that women's smaller brains were of adaptive significance. Today, this fact is more usually associated with relative body sizes (which may have adaptive significance), and that there is not necessarily a direct connection between brain volume and intellectual ability. Although this is not to deny that, in this respect, there may be some differences between male and female.

What I must note is that there is considerable biological debate today as to why sexuality exists, and even more particularly as to why it persists in the higher animals like mammals. Older explanations in terms of genetic benefits for the group (the species) are deemed incompatible with modern thought on the workings of selection. One suggestion indeed is that males in slower breeding species are redundant and persist only because biology has found no way of dispensing with them (Williams 1975). Another suggestion is that sex enables organisms to stay one step ahead of disease (Hamilton, Axelrod, and Tenese 1990). But, whatever the truth—and male parental care (as occurs in humans) does redress the balance somewhat—it is certainly the case that humans need both sexes to reproduce. We are not 'asexual'. Nor, incidentally, are we 'bisexual', in the biological sense of having functioning organs of both sexes (i.e. 'hermaphroditic'). If you like, we are a 'bisexual' species, in a sense apart from other senses of bisexuality to be considered shortly. But, we have and need two sexes.

Turning now from ultimate causes to proximate causes, it has long been known that males and females differ at the cellular level, specifically with respect to chromosomes. Humans have 46 chromosomes, two of which are the 'sex chromosomes'. In humans, unlike birds for instance, females are the 'homogametic' sex, meaning that they have similar ('X') chromosomes. Males are the 'heterogametic' sex, with one X chromosome, and one ('Y') somewhat shorter chromosome. It is this difference which triggers the growth into sexual differences as discussed above. Or, rather, it is the difference of the Y chromosome which somehow directs the creation of a male, for there seems to be at work something aptly named the 'Adam Principle'. All other things being equal, the developing fetus will grow up into a female. What makes things unequal is the fact that somehow the Y chromosome stimulates the production of two key substances, hormones: androgen and Mullerian-inhibiting factor. The former triggers the growth of male organs, and the latter represses the development of female organs (Money and Schwartz 1978). (See Figures 4.1 and 4.2.)

Sometimes, in both the professional and the popular literature, one sees the suggestion or claim that, given

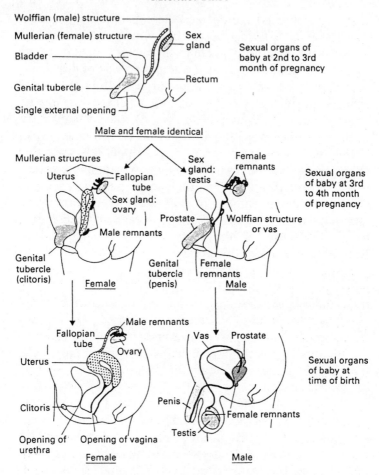

FIG. 4.1. Sexual differences in the human fetus

Note: The internal reproductive anlagen (early stages of the organs) are at the outset dually represented. The male and female organs have the same beginnings and are homologous with one another.
Source: Money and Schwartz 1978: 768.

our knowledge of the chromosomes, the real or true mark of sex difference lies at this level rather than that of gross physical anatomy/function. And indeed in some circles it is cytology which is taken as definitive. Olympic athletes, for instance, are required to take a chromosome

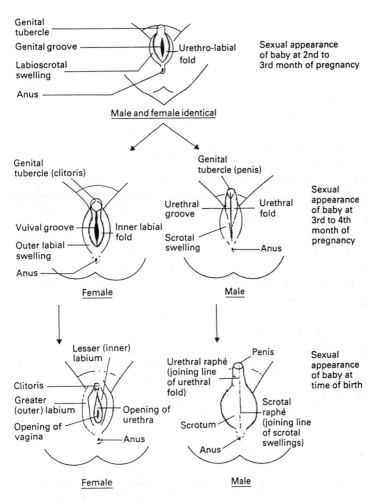

FIG. 4.2. External genital differentiation in the human fetus

Note: The external sex organs of male and female differentiate from the same anlagen and cannot be distinguished if a baby is born with differentiation unfinished.

Source: Money and Schwartz 1978: 768.

test. My own feeling is that to insist on cell difference as the essence of sexual difference, as a point of philosophy, is to take an outmoded Aristotelian approach to definition— one given a modern spin by a kind of reductionism. Only the truly small gives us the essence. All of the rest is accident.

At least, what one can say is that there are some real-life examples which (should) give this philosophy pause for thought. Although it is true that some people are physically on the boundary, 'hermaphrodites', there are also people who are boundary cases if (and sometimes only if) one looks at matters through a reductionist lens. Most notable are XY chromosome people who are androgen insensitive (Money and Ehrhardt 1972). They develop as girls, grow up as girls, and mature (without the need of any artificial hormone therapy) into women (Figure 4.3). Normally their condition comes to light only after they have attempted heterosexual intercourse, because their bodies' production of Mullerian inhibiting factor (MIF) has led to blockage of the vagina. Although these people are in fact sterile, I find it hard to argue that they are 'truly' males. What would this mean? That they should use the men's lavatories? That they should play for Arsenal? That, after a frustrating honeymoon, they should be told that their marriage is invalid and that, in God's eyes, they are guilty of a vile sin?

My feeling is that, as in most cases, the question of classification here is a pragmatic matter. It may well be that if one is trying to avoid cheating—a prime concern in the Olympics—chromosome tests are more stable. Perhaps also they are less open to ambiguity, although here also there are problems, for some people have very odd combinations of chromosomes. Does one want to say that someone with only one sex chromosome (it has to be an X) is not a real woman? Or what about someone who is XXY, or some other atypical combination? Because a classification is good for the Olympics, it does not follow that it has to be binding on us in other respects. Biologically and socially, with respect

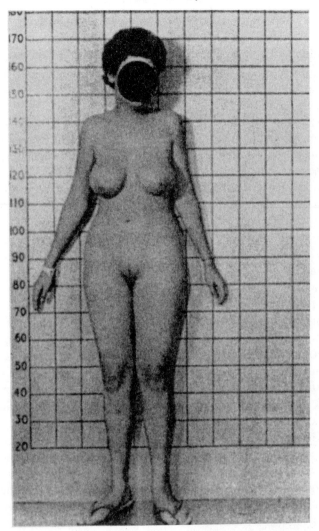

FIG. 4.3. Body morphology in an adult with the androgen-insensitivity syndrome

Note: Feminizing puberty occurs with no hormonal treatment needed, under the influence of oestrogens normally secreted by the testes in males since the body is unresponsive to the competitive effect of testicular androgen.
Source: Money and Ehrhardt 1972: 116.

71

to sex, what matters is not how things were caused, but how they end up. The shape and function of anatomical sex really counts.

Gender

We start to introduce the social alongside the biological, and as we do, we begin to move from sex as the purely functional, or the purely anatomical/physiological, to the internal aspects of sex, to the psychological and the behavioural and the cultural. Here, one of the most important terms to be introduced and defined is that of 'gender'. This refers to the sex with which one identifies, as well as (to some extent) the sex with which one conforms socially and behaviourally. One's gender refers to the sense that one has of being male or female (Ruse 1988).

Hence, whereas 'sex is between the legs, gender is between the ears' (Stein 1992: 335). To some degree, gender extends to one's sense of being 'masculine' or 'feminine', where these refer to gender emotions and actions more generally; although note that whatever the causes of gender, these latter terms are certainly somewhat bound up with culture. An Australian male may have a strong sense of his own male-ness, yet deplore much that passes for appropriate masculine behaviour in his society.

'Gender identity' is usually a term used of one's identification with persons of a physical sex. A 'transsexual' is some-one who feels a misfit, for their gender does not correspond to their sex. Apparently it is much more common in people with male sex organs—'I was a woman trapped in a man's body'. Inasmuch as it is ever appropriate to speak of 'luck' in such cases, here is an instance. Surgically, it is much easier to shape a male body into a female body, than conversely. I shall be coming shortly to the question of homosexuality, but as a general point one can stress that transsexuality is not to be confused with homosexuality. As a rule, homosexuals have a gender identity quite appropriate to their physical sex (Green 1974; Stoller 1968).

There is some considerable question about the causes of transsexuality. General opinion seems to be that one's sense of gender identity comes from imprinting in the first eighteen months or so of life (Money 1961). Little males are treated as little boys and little females as little girls—in the Guelph General Hospital they start off life with the appropriate blue or pink blankets. Children who are possessed of ambiguous genitalia seem not to have too much difficulty in gender image, so long as an early decision is made one way or the other, and then accepted consistently. Notoriously, there is a set of (biologically) male twins, one of whom lost his penis in a circumcision accident. He was reared, successfully, as a girl (Money and Schwartz 1978).

If decisions are delayed, then there is confusion and ambiguity. Transsexuals, often, have been raised somewhat inappropriately. At least, there do seem to be atypical patterns in family life. Males (the more common) tend to be very pretty or beautiful and have a very great identification with mother. Often they are encouraged to dress up as girls and discouraged from thinking of themselves as males. I think it fair to say, however, that the whole question is still mysterious, and no one would assert or deny categorically that biology might be involved. (I am not sure that the biologist would insist that biology must be involved, directly. After all, a capacity for imprinting is biological, and if this can do all that is needed, then so be it.)

One point which should be stressed is that the transsexual and the 'transvestite' are two different beings. The transvestite can have a perfectly secure gender identity. The transvestite is simply somebody who likes to dress in clothing appropriate to the opposite sex, for erotic purposes. It is important to include 'erotic'. If this is excluded, we simply have a 'cross-dresser'. Obviously, what counts as transvestism and cross-dressing are to a certain extent cultural. I doubt that today we would regard as crossdressing the clothing worn by women soldiers, but the good Victorians would undoubtedly have done so. Indeed, when I went to Canada thirty years ago, my university there regarded women in blue jeans with biblical suspicion. (Interestingly, the Victorians were in the habit of cross-dressing their young boys in a way that we today would think quite inappropriate.)

A point of some interest, for which I know of no causal explanation, is that transvestites are more often than not as heterosexual as anyone, and in males if anything with a somewhat stronger sex drive than is usual (Kinsey *et al.* 1948). I am not, however, suggesting that men with a flagging sex drive should don a bra and panties. That, apparently, is a *post hoc* fallacy.

Sexual orientation

I come now to the question of 'sexual orientation' in which context the term 'sexual identity' most often arises. By sexual orientation I refer to the sex (and most probably gender) of the kind of person to whom one is erotically attracted. I am not simply referring to behaviour, although I will agree that this is undoubtedly connected. Rather, I am referring to the object of one's lust, if I can use such a term without implying anything necessarily crude or improper. A good operational definition focuses on the object(s) of one's fantasies when one is masturbating, for here one escapes societal constraints and opportunities and so forth. A 'heterosexual' is someone whose sex objects are of a different sex from themselves. A 'homosexual' is someone whose sex objects are of the same sex. (For this reason, one ought to pronounce the first 'o' in homosexual as in 'dog' rather than 'home', for it derives from the Greek word for 'same' rather than the Latin for 'man'.)

Today, one sometimes sees the suggestion that the term 'orientation' should be replaced by 'preference' (Stein 1992). Essentially, the reason for this is that the latter term seems to allow for a greater degree of freedom than the former. A man or woman of homosexual preference would seem to be more in control of their own destiny than a man or woman of homosexual orientation. I worry about this suggestion for two reasons. First because it seems to confuse significant aspects of determinism and freedom. What one does is not a logical consequence of how one feels. Second, inasmuch as the suggestion is that one chooses one's objects of sexual fantasy, it seems to be just plain false. One does not even have the freedom to choose through the mediating force of extensive therapy—psychological, biochemical, or whatever. If we have learnt anything in this century, it is that turning homosexuals into heterosexuals is just not on. (And I assume the converse would hold also.)

This is not to deny that different aspects or intensities of sexual orientation/drive might not lead some people more easily to adopt certain life-styles rather than others. Simone de Beauvoir (1953) claimed that women's sexuality (*qua* orientation) was more diffuse than that of men. Perhaps so. It is certainly the case that calls for the adoption of a certain sexual life-style come more readily from militant female homosexuals (lesbians) than from males. Generally, it strikes males as slightly ludicrous to suggest that one prefer the sex of one's partners on political grounds.

Already this discussion is running into the problem that, apart from the assumption that we are talking of a topic of real human interest, it rather presupposes that one can talk meaningfully of a person with homosexual orientation and a person with heterosexual orientation, and that these are as clear-cut as—if not triangles and squares—then at least males and females. *Qua* orientation is it the case that 'bisexuals' are as rare as they are *qua* physical sexuality? Still the best source of information on these and related questions are the surveys conducted on human sexuality by Alfred Kinsey and his associates (1948, 1953) over forty years ago, and at once they quieten worries about significance and importance. Their finding, staggering then and still noteworthy now, is that (taken as a whole, and admittedly drawing on a sample of mainly white-collar Americans) same-sex activity is remarkably common. Indeed, up to 50 per cent of men had had some kind of same-sex encounter, and no less than 37 per cent had had sex to orgasm at some point during or after adolescence.

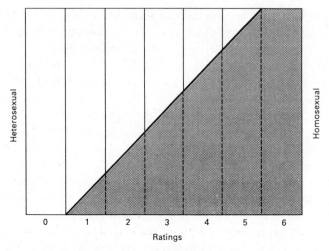

Based on both psychological reactions and overt experience, individuals rate as follows:

0 Exclusively heterosexual with no homosexual
1 Predominantly heterosexual, only incidentally homosexual
2 Predominantly heterosexual, but more than incidentally homosexual
3 Equally heterosexual and homosexual
4 Predominantly homosexual, but more than incidentally heterosexual
5 Predominantly homosexual, but incidentally heterosexual
6 Exclusively homosexual

FIG. 4.4. Heterosexual–homosexual rating scale

Source: Kinsey *et al.* 1948: 638, fig. 161.

But how does this break down? Are most people one or the other, or do they grade gradually from heterosexual to homosexual? According to Kinsey, the answer seems to be that it is a bit of both. The researchers devised a six-point scale, from exclusively heterosexual in activity and experience, to exclusively homosexual (Figure 4.4). Looking only at patterns of experience which lasted for more than three years, thereby excluding casual encounters and trying to get some true measure of feelings as well as activity, they found that most people (about 75 per cent) are exclusively heterosexual, that some people (about 5 per cent) are exclusively homosexual, and that the rest (about 20 per cent) are 'bisexual' in the sense that they like and engage in both heterosexual and homosexual acts, some more one way and some more the other (Figure 4.5).

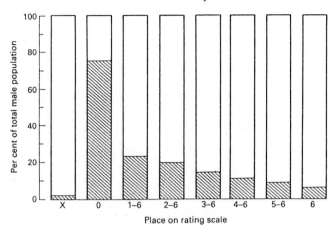

Fɪɢ. 4.5. Heterosexual–homosexual ratings in total male population (single and married) in any single year

Note: Passing experiences eliminated from data by showing only ratings which
have involved a period of at least 3 years after the males turned 16. Percentage
shown as 'X' have no socio-sexual contacts or reactions.
Source: Kinsey *et al.* 1948: 656, fig. 169.

I should say that these are figures which hold up pretty well
in other surveys, including surveys taken in different lands.[1] It
is also a pattern which is reflected in the Kinsey survey on the
female, although with significant differences, most notably
that lesbianism (especially in any intense sense) is far less
common than male homosexuality (Figure 4.6).

Among the females, the cumulative incidences of homosexual responses had ultimately reached 28 per cent; they had reached 50 per
cent in the males. The cumulative incidences of overt contacts to the
point of orgasm among the females had reached 13 per cent; among
the males they had reached 37 per cent. This means that homosexual responses had occurred in about half as many females as
males, and contacts which had proceeded to orgasm had occurred in

___

[1] Recent reports from Britain suggest that the incidence of male homosexuality is far lower than traditionally assumed, with as few as one male in ninety
being homosexual. Undoubtedly these claims will come under intense scrutiny,
but what one can say already is that the criteria of selection seem very stringent.
Some adolescent heterosexual or homosexual behaviour should not affect the
classification of adults.

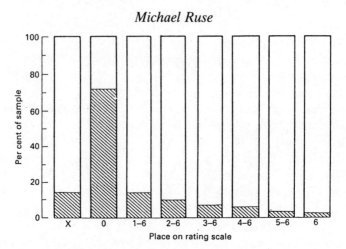

Fig. 4.6. Active incidence: heterosexual–homosexual ratings, single females, age 25

Note: This figure is not entirely comparable to fig. 4.5, since it tells only of single females, age 25. However, looking at all the data only confirms the fact that there are far fewer women than men involved in homosexual activities.
Source: Kinsey *et al.* 1953: 473, fig. 94.

about a third as many females as males. Moreover, compared with the males, there were only about a half to a third as many of the females who were, in any age period, primarily or exclusively homosexual. (Kinsey *et al.* 1953: 475)

One might perhaps suggest that here was a point where activity and inclination were pushed apart somewhat, more so than for men. Fifty years ago women had less control over their sexual destiny, and were more likely to be thrust into heterosexual liaisons than men, whatever their personal inclination. Also, not necessarily in opposition, we may have here an effect of the more diffuse nature of female sexuality (if such it be).

Are all senses of 'bisexuality' the same?

If you take Darwinism seriously, then homosexuality is an interesting phenomenon, because one seems not to have inclinations/actions promoting reproduction. But, although various models have been devised to explain its biological existence, it is not my end here simply to discuss homosexuality as an interesting human phenomenon (although I think it is) nor even do I want to survey all the things which have been said about or claimed for homosexuals as opposed to heterosexuals. As it happens, there is a lot of folklore both within and without the so-called 'professional' literature. Claims have been made about homo/heterosexual differences in body weight, body size, appearance, intelligence, birth order, life-style, employment preference, and much more (Ruse 1988). There may be some truth in some of these claims. There may not. Conceivably lesbians age more rapidly (whatever that means) than heterosexual women. No doubt male homosexuals occur disproportionately in the field of acting. After all, one would naturally go where one would feel most welcome. What we can say is that there are lots of counter-examples.

However, there is one putative difference which is of concern to me here. This is the claim that homosexuals show more cross-sex features than do heterosexuals. We are not now talking about strict gender identity. Rather, that in life-style and practices homosexuals move more across the sex divide than do heterosexuals. (Obviously most people most of the time do not cross over, otherwise there would be no divide.) The extreme claim is that, in sexual practice and inclination, homosexual emotion and action has crossed right over the divide. Perhaps this is close to a definition, but if so it is a fairly synthetic one in that one would not make it unless one thought it concordant with truly empirical facts about other aspects of heterosexual life.

I should say that in trying to answer this seemingly simple question, almost at once one runs into the host of definitional and empirical questions that seem to surround all discussions of homosexuality, not the least of which is that most people have their minds set firmly before you start on enquiry. For instance, researchers on a more recent Kinsey study on

TABLE 1.1. *Homosexuals' and heterosexuals' memories of themselves as children*

	Homosexual			Heterosexual		
	N	f	%	N	f	%
Male						
Considered a sissy as a child	72	48	67	35	1	3
Female						
Considered a tomboy as a child	56	39	70	43	7	16

N = total number of subjects
f = number responding positively
Source: Saghir and Robins 1973: 19, 193.

homosexuality in the 1970s found that it is an axiomatic truth among San Francisco real estate agents that male homosexuals make good clients, because their 'feminine' nature leads them to spend disproportionate time on house renovation and maintenance. Lesbians, to the contrary, are disliked because they are fractious 'slobs' (Bell and Weinberg 1978).

Cutting through the folk beliefs—which may, of course, be true—empirical studies do support some cross-gender activities and inclinations. Although I say at once that this is not true of everybody, nor does it hold in every respect. Most solidly established is the fact that, before adolescence, future homosexuals report (and were seen as) being more likely to engage in cross-gender activities. Many male homosexuals reported being considered a 'sissy'. Virtually no heterosexuals fell into this category. Similarly for lesbians and 'tomboyishness', although this finding is obviously interpretable in different ways, for there was a significant segment of heterosexual women who had been considered tomboys (Saghir and Robbins 1973) (Table 4.1).

For adults, the information is more difficult to interpret and is perhaps more clouded by cultural factors. One can say that homosexuals have tended to score more highly than do heterosexuals on tests designed to discern cross-gender features (Dahlstrom and Welsh 1960). However the tests used in the past do seem to be of the kind that would give apoplexy to any politically correct thinker today (Figure 4.7). Of course, this does not preclude the devising of tests which are more sensitive to today's concerns and mores, or that they might not throw up the same answer, whatever the politically correct thinker might deem seemly.

In a way, one might think that the answer to this question about gender differences is not that important. Interesting perhaps, but not that significant. And to an extent, this is true. But in another way, it is false, as is shown by the numbers who would challenge the truth of any gender-crossing claims. Interestingly, these challenges come from both ends of the spectrum, both from that which claims homosexuality is a vile affliction and illness, and from those who claim that homosexuality is no more than an alternative life-style. Let us dig into this a little more deeply.

Aetiology

There are various reasons why the cross-gender claims are attacked—showing perhaps a somewhat ambiguous attitude towards the claims and the hopes of feminists, today's male homosexual activists often decry attempts to label them as inadequate or woman-like—but the chief reason is clearly that just about every traditional causal explanation of homosexuality (not forgetting the various forms of sexual/gender bisexuality) start from the claim that psychically/biologically humans are bisexual, in the sense that they have the potential to go in either male or female ways (as opposed to the sense that adults are both). In blocking the cross-gender claims, the

True

I think I would like the work of a librarian.
I used to like drop-the-handkerchief.
I have often wished I were a girl. (Or if you
    are a girl) I have never been sorry that I
    am a girl.
I like poetry.
I would like to be a florist.
I would like to be a nurse.
I like collecting flowers or growing house
    plants.
I like to cook.
I used to keep a diary.
If I were a reporter I would very much like
    to report news of the theater.
I would like to be a journalist.
If I were an artist I would like to draw
    flowers.
I like "Alice in Wonderland" by Lewis Car-
    roll.

False

I like mechanics magazines.
My feelings are not easily hurt.
I do not have a great fear of snakes.
I daydream very little.
I have never had any breaking out on my
    skin that has worried me.
I like science.
I believe there is a Devil and a Hell in after-
    life.
I am entirely self-confident.
There never was a time in my life when I
    liked to play with dolls.

FIG. 4.7. Statements taken from the Masculine/Feminine scale of
the Minnesota Multiple Personality Index

Note: The first block supposedly tends to evoke a 'True' response from homosexuals, and the second block a 'False' response. This scale is designed to detect
cross-gender dispositions in adult homosexuals.
Source: Dahlstrom and Welsh 1960: 65.

critics hope to attack the underbelly of the traditional aetiologies.

It is not my aim here to offer detailed or synoptic discussions of putative causes of sexual orientation. I would say that no one suggestion yet seems to be overwhelmingly proven, and that in fact my sense—one which I suspect is shared by many more knowledgeable than I—is that there is no *one* cause. However, I will make brief mention here of what are perhaps the two best-known suggestions, both of which show how crucial is the notion of bisexuality in its various senses to proposed causes of sexual orientation. This will serve as a springboard to the ultimate and defining topic of my discussion, that of sexual identity.

The first hypothesis is the famous—notorious—claim by Freud (1905), that homosexuality results from an unresolved Oedipus complex. It was Freud's belief that we are in some sense serially bisexual, sliding in childhood development back and forth across a gender scale, as the male/female, masculine/feminine parts of our nature reveal themselves. (For instance, beginning life we are in the 'oral phase', fixated on mother. For boys, this is male/heterosexual behaviour. For girls, this is male/homosexual behaviour.) In mature development, males realize that there is an incest barrier against love of mother, and so they generalize out to other women. Homosexuals, unable to break from mother, respect the barrier by slipping back down into a female/ homosexual phase of development. (An analogous story is told for girls.)

The second hypothesis, rather trendy today, locates the origin of sexual orientation in different balances of vital bodily fluids, specifically in certain hormones (Dörner 1976; Ruse 1988). It seems fairly well established that in adult humans the hormones do not determine sexual orientation— at least, they cannot change it. But perhaps before birth, specifically at the time of the development of the hypothalamus (third to sixth month of fetal life), relative proportions of sex hormones are crucial determinants. Specifically, boys who get less testosterone than average grow up to be homosexual, and girls who get more than average do the same.

Obviously, both of these hypotheses, different as they are, see humans as sitting on a male/female (sex), masculine/ feminine (gender) continuum, and one's sexual orientation as being a function of precisely where one sits on that continuum. Logically, I suppose it is not necessary that one's overall personality and dispositions (gender inclinations and actions, especially) be connected to one's place on the continuum *qua* orientation; but, the expectation surely is that, since humans are such a package deal in so many respects, one might anticipate a connection. Certainly proponents of these hypotheses have had such anticipations. (Notoriously, Freud identified masculine and feminine with 'active' and 'passive', with implications for homosexuality. But as he himself later realized, you can make the connection without such a negative, culture-bound dichotomy.)

It is not my intent to promote either Freud or the hormone theorists. But I will say that I find unconvincing the arguments of their critics, inasmuch as they centre on the bisexuality claims. Against Freud, his critics argued that one must approach the individual holistically, and that therefore (almost logically) it is illicit to isolate aspects of sexuality and to try to categorize them or to compare male and female.

[We] see that sex in its entirety refers to the differentiation in the individuals as regards their contrarelated action systems of reproduction. Taking these considerations now in reverse order, we start from the fact that, insofar as concerns their reproductive action systems, individuals are of two contrarelated types. It is precisely this differentiation that constitutes the character of the sexes. Each of the two systems may be dissected into a multitude of structures, substances and functions, of which it is composed. The sex aspect of every one of these constituent parts is derived from the fact of its participation in the system as a whole. (Rado 1940: 180)

To which I can only say that this seems to me to be conceptually confused—a diesel engine and a petrol engine are different, but they both have cylinders—and empirically false. Masters and Johnson's (1966) well-known studies of sexu-

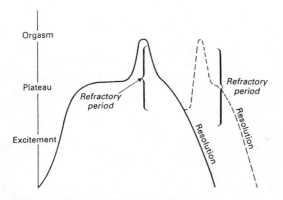

FIG. 4.8. The male sexual response cycle

Note: The broken line represents possible variations on the main theme.
Source: Masters and Johnson 1966: 5.

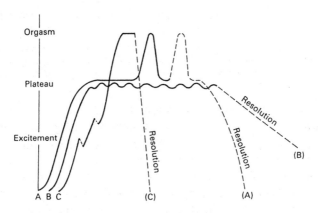

FIG. 4.9. The female sexual response cycle

Source: Masters and Johnson 1966: 5.

ality attempted to compare aspects of male and female sexuality, and without necessarily endorsing all of their conclusions, one can only say that not only do they seem to have been reasonably successful, but that their findings point to considerable overlap between men and women. Their comparison of the male/female orgasms makes the point (Figures 4.8 and 4.9).

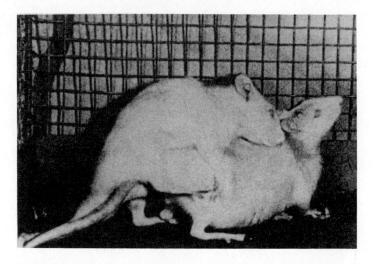

Fɪɢ. 4.10. Female rat mounting a male rat that is showing
lordosis

Note: The female was perinatally treated with testosterone propionate and the
male was castrated neonatally and substituted with androgen during adulthood.
A total sex hormone-dependent inversion of sexual behaviour is demonstrated.
Source: Dörner 1976: 170.

The criticism of the hormone (endocrinal) theory is somewhat more subtle. I should explain as background that the
theory's claims are very hard to test. Obviously, one cannot
experiment directly on fetal humans. Some of the strongest
indirect evidence comes from animal models, where it is certainly found that atypical hormonal levels (at appropriate
points of development) lead to sex-reversed behaviour. Male
rats, for instance, will perform 'lordosis', which is a kind of
crouching behaviour shown by a female during copulation
(Figure 4.10). In higher primates one has similar effects, and
I should point out that the concerned researchers are sensitive to the claim that their work has little to do with sexuality
per se.

If, for example, prenatal androgen induced new and bizarre types of
behaviour not usually found in rhesus males or females, or if it
introduced distortions in behaviour patterns usually displayed in

the same way by all rhesus, then the effects would have to be characterized as abnormalities. In such a circumstance, the studies might be useful as curiosities or as animal psychiatric models. This is not the manner in which the prenatal androgens work, however, and although we have studied intensively over the past decade as many as 30 different kinds of behavioral responses, we have never found behavior that was modified in the hermaphrodite that did not normally differ in its expression in normal males and normal females. In short, the action of prenatal androgen is limited to those behavioral patterns that are normally sexually dimorphic. (Goy *et al.* 1977: 149–50)

The argument by analogy, obviously, is that hormones in like manner affect the sexually dimorphic behaviour in humans, and thus one has an explanation of alternative sexual orientations. (I should say that other evidential arguments are offered, including known and supposed effects of hormones on humans. Recently, there have been claims about actual differences in the hypothalami of people with different orientations.)

The critics argue that it is simply illicit to argue that same-sex human behaviour—even more, same-sex human attractions—have anything to do with animal behaviour, even if one agrees (say) that a male rat performing lordosis is showing female rat behaviour. What right has one to say, for instance, that two males engaged in anal intercourse are in some sense exhibiting the behaviour shown by a man and a woman engaged in vaginal intercourse? Even less, what right has one to say that the emotions are the same?

In reply to which I can only say that while the behaviours may not be exactly the same, they are not all that different either, and the differences are rather forced on one by matters of anatomy. I am not claiming that both males (say) are showing female behaviour, but, at least one is, inasmuch as it is anatomically possible. It is not as if male homosexuals' idea of a good time is merely that of (for instance) going for a vigorous run together, without thought of body contact or ejaculation.

87

There is, of course, a leap from behaviour to emotions. I, for one, would feel very uncomfortable about jumping straight from hormonally manipulated rats to the passion of David for Jonathan. However, even here I cannot see why one should bar a priori any claims about cross-gender characteristics. One should not say that male homosexuals simply show female emotions, or conversely. Apart from anything else, the remarkable sexual activity of males as opposed to females suggests strongly that members of both sexes, whatever their orientations, retain certain features, exclusively. But a male's sexual lust being triggered by the form of another male—with subsequent fantasies, inclinations, activities—does not strike me as in principle different from that of women in a similar situation. After all, women are turned on by men's features, and the triggers do tend to be faces, bodies, actions, ways of talking, and so forth. There is no accounting for taste, but females do not normally wait until their partner performs well in a dialect of Swahili before they get aroused. The same is true of male homosexuals.

Homosexuality as a social construction

Digging more deeply, one asks why people would want to deny that people with a homosexual orientation are exhibiting cross-gender activity/emotion. In the case of the Freudian critics, the answer is easy. For Freud, homosexuality is less an abnormality than an immaturity. As such, it is not open to change through therapy, because in itself there is nothing wrong. The critics feel that it is a vile affliction, and therefore can and must be changed. They have a vested interest, therefore, in denying the whole Freudian bisexual schema, and in categorizing homosexuality as something totally alien to humankind. They could hardly regard sympathetically the idea that homosexuals are merely exhibiting behaviour/emotions shared by almost half the human race—and that they might be happy in so doing!

The more recent critics, those who attack endocrinal hypotheses, have a very different axe to grind. They want to go completely the other way, arguing that such hypotheses, like any of the traditional hypotheses (including Freud's), are simply conceptually mistaken: this is just the wrong way entirely to approach homosexuality, or heterosexuality for that matter. Since the attack of Freud's critics seems to have collapsed in on itself—apart from anything else, not one seems to have had any real success whatsoever in changing sexual orientation—I shall deal no more with it here. But the recent critics are today in full cry, so it is to their own position that I now turn.

Basically the claim is that traditional approaches mistakenly regard homosexuality (and heterosexuality) as a thing, waiting to be explained. It is given ontological status akin to trees which exist in forests when no one is around. But this is to go wrong right at the beginning, for homosexuality does not—cannot—have this ontological status. Homosexuality is a human phenomenon, and since humans are social beings, it is a social phenomenon. Moreover, since it is a phenomenon of society, it is a construction of society, and hence since societies vary, it will vary.

The particular interrelations and activities which exist at any moment in a specific society create sexual and other categories which, ultimately, determine the broad range of modes of behavior available to individuals who are born within that society. In turn, the social categories and interrelations are themselves altered over time by the activities and changing relationships of individuals. Sexual categories do not make manifest essences implicit within individuals, but are the expression of the active relationships of the members of entire groups and collectives. (Padgug 1979: 56)

The most powerful and influential of the 'social constructivist' writings on this topic came from the pen of the late Michel Foucault.

As defined by the ancient civil or canonical codes, sodomy was a category of forbidden acts; their perpetrator was nothing more than the juridical subject of them. The nineteenth-century homosexual became a personage, a past, a case history, and a childhood, in addition to being a type of life, a life form, and a morphology, and indiscreet anatomy and possibly a mysterious physiology. Homosexuality appeared as one of the forms of sexuality when it was transposed from the practice of sodomy onto a kind of interior androgyny, a hermaphroditism of the soul. The sodomite had been a temporary aberration; the homosexual was now a species. (Foucault 1978: 43)

One should say that this perspective is one which has been widely accepted and used by historians of sexuality—producing, in my opinion, some of the most exciting work in recent years. It has also found (some) favour in the philosophical community. Ian Hacking, for one, has tried to generalize out from social categories like 'homosexual' and 'deviant', to a position which he calls 'dynamic nominalism'—'putting some flesh on that wizened figure, John Locke' (Hacking 1986: 87)—where such categories are seen as inventions or constructions of some kind.

Let me take even the vibrant Hobbes, Goodman, and their scholastic predecessors as pale reflections of a perhaps nonexistent static nominalist, who thinks that all categories, classes, and taxonomies are given by human beings rather than by nature and that these categories are essentially fixed throughout the several eras of humankind. I believe that static nominalism is doubly wrong: I think that many categories come from nature, not from the human mind, and I think our categories are not static. A different kind of nominalism—I call it dynamic nominalism—attracts my realist self, spurred on by theories about the making of the homosexual and the heterosexual as kinds of persons by my observations about official statistics. The claim of dynamic nominalism is not that there was a kind of person who came increasingly to be recognized by bureaucrats or by students of human nature but rather that a kind of person came into being at the same time as the kind itself was being invented. In some cases, that is, our classifications and our classes conspire to emerge hand in hand, each egging the other on. (Hacking 1986: 78)

In conjunction with this kind of philosophy—and here, at last, I tie in my essay with my title—one often sees the suggestion that the term 'sexual orientation' should be abolished. One should rather speak of people playing a 'sexual role' and of having a 'sexual identity'. Thus one should not speak of '*the* homosexual' or '*a* homosexual', or of someone having a 'homosexual orientation'. Rather, in a certain society, people play certain sexual roles and have (adopt, are given, are forced into) certain sexual identities.

'Homosexual' and 'heterosexual' *behavior* may be universal; homosexual and heterosexual *identity and consciousness* are modern realities. These identities are not inherent in the individual. In order to be gay, for example, more than individual inclinations (however we might conceive of those) or homosexual activity is required; entire ranges of social attitudes and the construction of particular cultures, subcultures, and social relations are first necessary. To 'commit' a homosexual act is one thing: to *be* a homosexual is something entirely different. (Padgug 1979: 58–9)

I should add also, although I do not pretend to speak for everyone who is a constructivist, that along with the historical/epistemological claims, one often finds an underlying sociological claim. That the creation of beliefs that homosexuality is a 'thing' which calls for explanation was a deliberate act, whereby one group of people sought to exercise power over another group, as the first group 'identified' the second group as a category of less-than-desirable status.

A proliferation of sexualities through the extension of power; an optimization of the power to which each of these local sexualities gave a surface of intervention: this concatenation, particularly since the nineteenth century, has been ensured and relayed by the countless economic interests which, with the help of medicine, psychiatry, prostitution, and pornography, have tapped into both this analytical multiplication of pleasure and this optimization of the power that controls it. (Foucault 1978: 22)

Ontology and other matters

Let me suggest straight off that I think this a position of considerable interest and importance. I have made reference already to the historiographic gains and I believe there is philosophical potential here also. Nor do I intend to damn the view with faint praise, for I intend to take it seriously by pointing to places of ambiguity and by criticizing some of its more dubious assumptions, with an end to accepting that which is valid. And as a first move, I would point to an ambiguity in precisely what is being claimed. Sometimes, in the more extreme form, the argument seems to be directed to the conclusion that homosexuality (and heterosexuality) do not really exist at all. They are just social constructions, and as such are fictions, and as such are non-existent. Whether this was truly Foucault's view, certainly many have taken him to have said this.

I will take it without much discussion that this is not really a very satisfactory line of argument. Even if homosexuality is not a thing like a chair or a table, this does not mean that it is non-existent. As I pointed out at the beginning, the US Constitution is not a thing like a chair or a table. Yet it certainly exists. And in any case, the simple empirical fact of the matter is that there are people who are labelled 'homosexual' and who indeed identify themselves as 'homosexual'. 'Shout it loud! I'm gay and proud!'

Homosexuality exists in some sense. But in what sense? Would one say that it is 'just' a social category? Well, yes, but I am not sure why one has to put in the 'just'. The answer, I suppose, is that it is just a social category in a way that biological sex was not. Robinson Crusoe on his island alone was male. He could not be masculine, let alone homosexual—at least, not until Man Friday turned up. Yet is this all that we—anyone—would want to say? Certainly, this is the impression in some writings, especially from those who would separate us off from animal sexuality and from any hint that our sexuality is confined to a scale.

If we compare human sexuality with that of other species, we are immediately struck by its richness, its vast scope, and the degree to which its potentialities can seemingly be built upon endlessly, implicating the entire human world. Animal sexuality, by contrast, appears limited, constricted, and predefined in a narrow physical sphere.

This is not to deny that human sexuality, like animal sexuality, is deeply involved with physical reproduction and with intercourse and its pleasures. Biological sexuality is the necessary precondition for human sexuality. But biological sexuality is only a precondition, a set of potentialities, which is never unmediated by human reality, and which becomes transformed in qualitatively new ways in human society. The rich and ever-varying nature of such concepts and institutions as marriage, kinship, 'love,' 'eroticism,' in a variety of physical senses and as a component of fantasy and religious, social, and even economic reality, and the general human ability to extend the range of sexuality far beyond the physical body, all bear witness to this transformation. (Padgug 1979: 50–1)

Does this mean that everything is social? That society somewhat arbitrarily picks out certain people and labels them as 'homosexual', as it labels others 'heterosexual'? Surely not! Does anyone want to say that one's inclinations are purely a function of societal labelling? The point is that we have these inclinations, whatever society might say. Although this is not to say that society might not be a factor in causing these inclinations. (I think now of a society like classical Greece, where in the upper classes there was a rigid separation of the sexes before marriage.)

Another tack is that, although the inclinations exist, and are themselves more than just labelling, the calling of someone a 'homosexual' is a purely societal phenomenon. In this sense, sexual categories are unreal or artificial. But here again it is necessary to separate out the dross from the gold. It is true that, without a society, one would not call someone a 'homosexual'. This is trivial. What is not trivial, but is true and significant, is that the full implications of what it means to call someone a 'homosexual' is in important part a function of society. Homosexuality in England in the 1950s had implications of sickness and criminality that it does not have now.

Yet—and here I think the more moderate constructivist like Hacking would agree—the claim cannot be that *qua* orientation (inclinations, activities) we are all the same, essentially bisexual, and society (although it does not create the inclinations) arbitrarily picks out some of us rather than others. Although I would not deny that people sometimes get labelled on less than complete information, the Kinsey studies show that there is a spectrum, and that some people come more at one end and some more at the other. Indeed, the social constructivists themselves have relied on this very point, showing (truly) that whatever else one should not think of homosexuality and heterosexuality as clear-cut categories like triangles and squares (McIntosh 1968).

The point is that orientation seems to be a given, and then society does with it what it does. But what does this entail? I detect at least two responses in the social constructivist literature. The first response is that although our orientations are thrust upon us, they are thrust upon us by society. Some societies (because of what they are) have people all at one end of the Kinsey scale. Other societies have people scattered up and down the scale. Yet other societies have people polarized at the ends. As you can imagine, classical Greece is the example usually trotted out here, as a society with a very different spread to our own. Important to this line of argument is the implication that—using Greece as the example— some societies simply have empty the category of 'homosexual' in the sense (i.e. Kinsey 6) that we have, as also they (or others) have empty the category of 'heterosexual' in the sense (Kinsey 0) that we have.

To which argument, the following points apply. First, note that we seem to have slipped back into considering homosexuality as a 'thing'. Societally caused, maybe. But a thing, nevertheless. Second, following on the first point, one would like some evidence as to how this thing comes about. Perhaps society does make for homosexual orientations. Give us a line of evidence. I am not now saying that it is in no way true. I expect that society does have some influence. I can imagine that if there were no girls around, young men might fall for pretty boys (Dover 1978). I just want the evidence spelled out.

Third, surely no one would claim that society could make everyone exclusively homosexual. Certainly, no one who has any knowledge of modern biology. No evolutionist could agree that natural selection is that easy going. Fourth, and most importantly, note that we have an empirical claim about societies, and that in particular there are supposedly societies significantly different from ours. At which point, I must note also that—notwithstanding the exciting historical work of the social constructivists—today's most distinguished historian of homosexuality, John Boswell (1980), argues strongly that societies of the past, in ancient times and in medieval times, in the West and in the Arab world, have all had people who were clearly identifiable as homosexual (*sensu* Kinsey 6). Conversely, I must note that the constructivists, with Foucault at their fore, have tended not to provide detailed historical evidence across the ages to back their claims. Nor have they provided counter-evidence to anthropological studies which find people with (nigh exclusive) homosexual orientations in non-Western, often pre-literate societies.

The second response, in the social constructivist literature to the fact that orientation seems to be a given, is that no one would really want to claim that society makes for the orientations, anyway. Rather, it is in the very act of labelling someone a 'homosexual' that society makes its chief input. This is certainly not a necessary phenomenon. There could be and have been societies with Kinsey 6s, where no one has taken the slightest interest. They have had an exclusively homosexual orientation, but have not been 'homosexuals'. It is in this sense that homosexuality is a construction, and of course it is in this sense that the power thesis becomes important. The 'homosexual' was invented to control a group of people. As Hacking would say, 'homosexuality' was not just an arbitrary invention out of thin air. The construction and the reality somehow come together at this point. But there was construction, nevertheless.

Actually, as Hacking himself realizes, in the case of homosexuality (as opposed to, say, the person with a split personality) there has to be more to the story than this.

Suppose there is some truth in the labelling theory of the modern homosexual. It cannot be the whole truth, and this for several reasons, including one that is future-directed and one that is past-directed. The future-directed fact is that after the institutionalization of the homosexual person in law and official morality, the people involved had a life of their own, individually and collectively. As gay liberation has amply proved, that life was no simple product of the labelling.

The past-directed fact is that the labelling did not occur in a social vacuum, in which those identified as homosexual people passively accepted the format. There was a complex social life that is only now revealing itself in the annals of academic social history. It is quite clear that the internal life of innumerable clubs and associations interacted with the medico-forensic-journalistic labelling. At the risk of giving offence, I suggest that the quickest way to see the contrast between making up homosexuals and making up multiple personalities is to try to imagine split-personality bars. Splits, insofar as they are declared, are under care, and the syndrome, the form of behavior, is orchestrated by a team of experts. Whatever the medico-forensic experts tried to do with their categories, the homosexual person became autonomous of the labelling, but the split is not. (Hacking 1986: 83–4)

This concurs with a worry that I have also, about whether it is in fact historically true that people at some point in time were labelled 'homosexual' but not before. This is quite apart from another of my worries about the supposed involvement of the medical profession and others. Again, I note that Boswell (1982) thinks there were people labelled 'homosexual' before the modern era. I note also that, for apparently so deliberate an act, there seems to be considerable ambiguity about when it happened. At the end of the seventeenth, eighteenth, or nineteenth centuries? All options have been offered. (See Foucault 1978; Weeks 1977; Davidson 1987;

Dynes 1988.) And while it is not my practice to offer unqualified praise of the medical profession, I would point out finally that—power or not—in our age its efforts have been a major factor in the liberation of today's homosexuals from the oppressions of the past.

Homosexual identity

So where do I come out at the end? I have said that my attitude towards social constructivism is not merely one of criticism and denial. Whether or not society is a causal factor in people's orientations—and I myself expect that it is—I would certainly agree that society plays a significant role in what we mean by 'homosexual', where meaning refers to more than just a dictionary definition and to the wider sense of how we think of a homosexual. Sinner? Criminal? Pervert? Sick? Talented? Fun to be with? To be excluded? Not to be excluded? The sort of thing we would think of when hiring? The sort of thing we would not think of when hiring? The sort of thing we would think of when hiring, but counsel ourselves not to think of when hiring? Important? Not important? A subject for philosophical discussion?

I would argue that in the light of this realization, there is a good place for the term 'homosexual identity', or more generally for the term 'sexual identity'. I would not use it as a synonym for 'sexual orientation'. This latter I would leave in the sense defined earlier, referring to inclinations, and inasmuch as there are disembodied things in these cases, as referring to something at that ontological level. (Orientations are hardly that disembodied. The form of one's inclinations and fantasies will be societally moulded. Americans, for instance, thanks to their obsession with personal hygiene, can be far more oral than the rest of us.)

Rather I would propose 'sexual identity' for the sense that one has of one's sexuality, as conferred on one by one's orientation, as society regards people of one's orientation, and—this is important because it shows that I allow a dimension of freedom most social constructivists fear their critics deny—as one decides to act given one's orientation and societal norms. Thus a person with a heterosexual orientation who behaves and lives openly heterosexually has a heterosexual identity. A person with a homosexual orientation, who behaves and lives openly homosexually has a homosexual identity. And the same applies to the bisexual, using this term now to refer to people in the middle of the gender/behaviour scale.

Yet there are people whose orientations and identities do not match. You might say that the person with a homosexual orientation who is passing as heterosexual should truly be regarded as one who has a heterosexual identity, as they are thus regarded by society. In a sense, it is all a matter of words and the words are not fixed here. You might say that if people want to be regarded as having a certain sexual identity, that is their choice and there is no higher authority. But, I would rather say that this person is playing a heterosexual 'role' but that their identity is divided—confused perhaps, but not necessarily. In this way, my use of 'sexual identity' bears a strong analogy to the fairly well-established notion of 'gender identity' in that they both include a sense of self. I prefer consistency to what I think is a false sense of personal autonomy. But as I have said, these are matters of words, and I would be the last to say that words are unimportant. Perhaps others can persuade me to change my preferred usage.

Just let me say in conclusion—having tried hard in this essay to stay away from moral directives—that the important thing is not to insist that people relinquish a divided identity (using terms in my sense), let alone attempt to change an identity which we do not share. Rather it is to work for a society where people can feel free to work out their identities as they will. For as we have seen, sexual identity is a reality. As it is also a construct.

5

Fictional Identities

TERENCE CAVE

A philosophical fiction

Bernard Williams begins his essay in this volume with a quotation from a novel, Derek Parfit with one of his notorious science fiction examples.[1] I begin more soberly with a fragment from the writings of Pascal (I have taken some liberties with the gender of the pronouns, for reasons which will be explained shortly):

What is the self? [Qu'est-ce que le moi?]

Imagine someone who goes to the window to look at people walking past. If I walk past, am I entitled to say that she went to the window to look at me? No; because she isn't thinking of me in particular.

I should like to express my gratitude to the Board of Management for the Herbert Spencer Lectures for inviting me to participate in this series. They could hardly have chosen a more topical theme, nor a more explosive one. The social and political issues that turn on the question of identity are, as the millenium draws to a close, as fundamental as they have ever been. It therefore seems a pity that the team of speakers was so culturally uniform—all male, all white, four out of six from Oxford. It is clear that the selection was made according to a principle which is often invoked in such circumstances, namely that, in the disinterested pursuit of truth, gender and ethnic origin are irrelevant. Yet identity is the one concept which cannot, unless one is a hard-line metaphysician, transcend all individual and cultural perceptions. Once you ask the question of identity, you have to address particularity and difference. In the materials I work with, certainly, experience is always prior, and truth is only conceivable in particular forms. I am therefore personally sorry—with all due respect to the other contributors to this volume—that our collective identity is not more varied.

[1] See above, pp. 1 and 2; also Williams 1991: 2ff., and Parfit 1984: 199ff.

But imagine that someone loves a person because of his good looks: does she love *him*? No, because if he catches smallpox, which destroys the good looks without killing the person, she will cease to love him.

And if someone loves me for my judgement, for my memory, does she love *me*? No, because I can lose these qualities without losing my self.

Where then is this 'self' of mine, if it is neither in the body nor in the soul? And how is it possible to love the body or the soul other than for these qualities, which cannot be what constitutes the self, since they are perishable? For would anyone love the substance of someone's soul in abstract, regardless of that person's qualities? That is impossible, and would also be unfair. Thus one never loves anyone as a person; one can only love qualities.

We should therefore no longer sneer at people who require others to honour them for their rank or office; for what we love in other people is never anything other than sham qualities.[2]

I do not offer this passage as an exemplary definition of what Pascal calls 'le moi' and what we might call personal identity: few readers will find it easy to accept Pascal's quasi-Cartesian presupposition of an essential and imperishable 'I', entirely distinct from all the 'qualities' that become associated with it, including memory.

I offer it first of all as an example occupying the borderline between strictly philosophical argument and fiction: much of what I have to say will be on or near that borderline, even though I approach it from the fictional side (more generally, the literary side). Pascal's opening move, placing a third-person observer at a window and then supposing that his or her glance falls on a first-person passer-by, is already a precisely structured fiction in miniature: one could easily imagine it as the opening of a novel or short story. An amorous

---

[2] Pascal 1963: 591 (fr. 688). In the phrase 'qualités empruntées', translated here as 'sham qualities', the word 'empruntées' literally means 'borrowed', hence 'assumed', as in the expression 'an assumed name' ('un nom emprunté'); Pascal's final sentence thus introduces overtones of impersonation, or fictitious identity.

development is then sketched in, taking a rather gruesome turn; and the socio-political theme of the final sentence could also quite easily be converted into fiction: the relative values of political honour and love are after all a well-tried theme of both canonic and tabloid fiction, from *Antony and Cleopatra* to present-day scandals resulting in the resignation of ministers. There is even a sting in the tail of the argument, like the twist at the end of a short story. The first reason why I changed the pronouns was to sharpen these narrative implications.

Now this pseudo-Pascalian story would be one in which identity was put to the test by means of a number of complex ethical dilemmas. It would present identity as a *relation*—as the problematic conjunction of an inward sense of self with the perceptions and judgements of others; it would also suggest a pessimistic view of identity in the sense that what others identify in us is shown to be something hollow and imaginary. All these themes will be relevant to my argument.

I could of course have used other examples of philosophical fictions: Locke's story of Prince Maurice and the parrot, Thomas Reid's story of the flogged boy, the brave captain and the amnesiac general, or Bernard Williams's hypothetical case, in his essay 'Are persons bodies?', of a certain Mary who isn't quite *the* Mary who would be the ideal object of one's love, but a rather faded copy, whom one loves because she's the best available.[3] The structure of Williams's analysis of this example is in fact not unlike Pascal's, and he even concludes in similar vein: 'Much of what we call loving a person would begin to crack under this.' In other words, he argues that a narrative about the ordinary-life experience of love can provide a powerful test case for where identity lies, his conclusion in this case being that it is not easy to do without bodies.

[3] Williams 1991: 81. For those unfamiliar with the history of philosophical debate on identity in the English language, an anthology of texts is provided by Perry 1975.

This particular fragment of philosophical fiction has been chosen, then, in order to launch some of the themes of this essay from a particular angle. I next want to consider it as an instance of *textual* identity: this is a topic which strictly speaking lies outside the realm of fictional identities, but it will allow an essential methodological point to be introduced.

Textual identity

The Pascal fragment is easily detachable because the *Pensées* do not form a continuous sequence of sustained arguments. It has its own heading or title, and the argument it presents, although extremely concise and sketchy, appears to be complete. It has, one might say, its own identity.

To say that Pascal is 'mistaken', that his thinking is, from our vantage point, confused or erroneous, becomes inappropriate if the fragment is looked at from this angle (which does not mean that one must remain wholly indifferent to its implications). One would instead want to gather together a set of textual and historical co-ordinates which would make it possible to identify as precisely as possible that particular perception; to identify it as peculiarly Pascalian; and to identify it more broadly as bearing the signature of the writer's time and culture.

The example is a convenient one, because it is short and self-contained enough to raise the question: what is the identity of a text? How much text do we need in order to be able to say that it has this kind of identity? Such questions are even more clearly put by instances where the authorship of the text, or its precise historical or cultural provenance, is uncertain; they arise, too, in cases of literary forgery and of pastiche. They are of course familiar to literary historians, and not only in notorious cases like Homer, Shakespeare, and Ossian; one is always asking questions such as 'What is it in a given novel or even a given sentence by Jane Austen that is distinctive of her writing?'

One could say here, I think, that the identity of a text is analogous to the identity of a person in so far as both may become the object of detective work, of identifying procedures: in this way, the problem of textual identity becomes a special variant of the question whether a person can adequately be identified in the absence of a body; indeed, not only in the absence of a body, but also without any possibility of ever recovering one. It is perhaps akin to imagining that one might be able to encounter a disembodied fragment of someone's personality and asking oneself how far it would be possible to identify a whole person on the basis of that fragment.

A more specific version of this text-person analogy is the sense in which the identity of a person may be structured like that of a fictional narrative (or vice versa). The question here would turn on the way in which narrative structure organizes and welds together materials which might otherwise seem unrelated or even incompatible. I leave it there for the moment, but will return to it later.

My main object at this stage is rather to bring out the methodological point that literary study obliges one to attend very carefully not only to what is being said but also to where it is coming from. In this sense, literary study is much closer to anthropology than it is to philosophy. It does not try to give a general answer to questions like 'what is personal identity?' It seeks to understand different, even alien, identities without reducing their difference: the identities in question being those of texts, of writers, and, more widely, of the tangled but already structured cultural context from which they are derived. Literature is a place of many voices, and of many kinds of voice.

This is the second reason why I altered Pascal's pronouns. In late twentieth-century English, they would have sounded awkward and evasive. Of course, a translator might decide to keep the awkwardness, but I wanted to intervene in this case in order to show that as soon as I engage with an alien textual voice I bring into play my own voice and *its* traces of identity.

Sounding out that difference and thinking about what it implies for both identities is again, I think, central to literary study.

The inward turn

Pascal's question and the kind of answer he gives are precisely datable: eighty years after the first edition of Montaigne's *Essays*, twenty years or so after Descartes's *Discourse on Method*, and immediately before an extraordinary flowering of French literature in which fictions of identity drawing on insights similar to Pascal's play a prominent part. This phenomenon itself belongs to a wider European development which is referred to by other contributors to this volume, a gradual but decisive shift in the way that identity is perceived.[4]

Crudely put, one could say that a predominantly outward set of co-ordinates for identity (social, political, religious) loses ground in favour of an almost obsessive attempt to locate identity in an interior self. This interior or subjective self may be many things: it may in the philosophical world be a pure Cartesian ego, or the point through which flows, in phenomenological accounts, the stream of *cogitationes*; it has become the subject of post-Freudian psychoanalysis and of various methods of psychiatric treatment; in a world closer to common experience, it is more likely to be the subject (the first-person singular narrator) of autobiographical narrative. As a *locus* of identity, it may best be thought of as a kind of elastic bag of idiosyncrasies, personal habits, private memories, private stories, or private fictions. A subjective sense of identity has no doubt been available to other cultures, and to

---

[4] A history of philosophy, a history of ideas, or a historical archaeology in the manner of Foucault would all show that the terms in which the nature of personal identity has been perceived underwent a major shift in what is loosely called the early modern period; this is the ground charted most recently in Taylor 1992.

earlier phases in our own: what we seem to have invented is this indefinitely extensible *filling up* of identity. The aim is saturation, total colonization of the terrain of the ego: identity is no longer what is sufficient or necessary to the interpersonal economy on which all societies depend.

This well-known history has a direct bearing on the question of fiction and fictional identities. The shift from plots dependent mainly on external action to what are loosely called 'psychological' plots (in which individuation of character is central) is a fundamental aspect of the history of European literature in the seventeenth and eighteenth centuries: contemporaries who wrote treatises on poetics were fully aware of it. It is perhaps not an accident that it appears first in drama, the genre which depends on impersonation; but narrative fiction soon takes over as its primary vehicle. The novel thrives on the proliferation of particulars, both external and internal; and the rise of the novel is synonymous with the rise of the modern fictional character, whose identity is highly individualized and who is often a first-person narrator embarked on a restless search for an adequate sense of self. One could well argue, in fact, that the history of identity is a good deal more visibly and colourfully exhibited in fiction than in philosophy as such. It is also exhibited *par excellence* in the fact that autobiography and autobiographical fictions flourish in tandem from the eighteenth century onwards.

This historical commonplace opens up a crucial issue in the broader understanding of identity. It would obviously be absurd to believe that the inward turn has replaced other ways of constructing identity. One might rather say that what we have here, displayed along a historical axis, is a delicate and difficult balance in the construction of individual identity: the balance between internal and external co-ordinates or criteria; between personal identity as individual differentiation and personal identity as constituted by belonging to one or more groups (family, gender, social status, national allegiance, ethnic affiliation, language, colour, and so on). Whether one is thinking of Sophocles' Theban trilogy or of the novels of Virginia Woolf, these apparently antithetical poles coexist.

We are touching here, then, on the large question of the way in which singular personal identity intersects with group identity—the question raised by Bernard Williams when he speaks of the narrow dividing line between identity achieved through belonging to a group and the loss of identity in a stereotype.[5] Now I think it is important in this context to avoid making—as Williams seems to, and as Strawson does at one point in his book *Individuals* (Strawson 1990: 112–15)—what might seem a logical move: namely, to say that personal identity must in the end be defined in contradistinction to membership of a group. Thus Strawson uses analogies from war and from cricket (sporting and military examples seem to play a prominent role in the discussion of identity by philosophers) to suggest that personal identity *disappears* when someone functions as a member of a group: he or she becomes, not an individual person, but—say—'square leg'.

This seems to me to be wrong, except in extreme cases like indoctrination and brainwashing and highly normative forms of military discipline. Square leg as a position on the diagram of a cricket pitch implies no personal individuation, but when Ian Botham or Waqar Younis or my sister plays square leg, they don't become ciphers; their own characteristics—agility, a sense of humour, aggression, their way of standing, the hat they like to wear and how they wear it, and so forth—determine their perceived performance. Inversely, and more importantly for my argument, their participation in such roles is a constituent part of their identity: performing as square leg, or first viola, or being a member of a political party, may become a non-trivial aspect of the way individuals perceive themselves and the way they are perceived *as an individual* by others. Belonging to a certain family and having a certain skin colour are even more clearly circumstances which may be fully internalized as a part of the structure of an individ-

---

[5] See above, p. 8.

V:

B William	1	2	3.	4.	5	6	7	8	9	10	11.	12	13	14.	15.	16.	17.	18	19.	20
D Ranjit	21.	22	23	24	25	26	27	28.	29	30.	31	32	33	34.	35	36	37.	38	39.	40
	41	42	43	44	45	46	47	48	49	50.	51	52	53	54	55.	56	57	58	59	60.
	61	62	63	64	65	66	67	68	69	70.	71	72	73	74	75	76,	77	78.	79.	80
M Rose	81	82	83	84	85	86	87	88	89	90.	91,	92	93,	94.	95	96	97,	98	99	100
T Cane	101	102.	103	104.	105,	106	107	108	109	110	111	112	113	114	115,	116,	117	118	119	120
	121	122	123	124	125	126	127	128	129	130	131	132	133	134	135,	136	137	138	139,	140
A D Smith	141	142,	143	144	145	146	147	148	149	150	151	152	153	154	155	156	157	158	159	160

H. Harris

ual's identity: they are not external factors added to an already distinct person. Of course it is true that personal identity may be manifested by a resistance to or rebellion against the imposition of some form of collective identity, but that clearly does not constitute a valid counter-argument.[6]

If pushed to its limits, this analysis demolishes most if not all of the internal/external opposition itself. Individual persons have no given, natural identity (except in so far as it is determined by their genetic code);[7] their individuality is progressively formed from layer upon layer of internal*ized* elements, language acquisition being just one example among many of this process. The individual begins to be socialized, and the social individualized, as soon as a person is born. The subjective perception of that identity is obviously different from its perception by others, just as the subjective perception of the body and its movements is different from the way others perceive that same body; but this is surely a relational difference, not a metaphysical one.

I am aware that these remarks open up an enormous philosophical can of worms. Their most notorious ancestor is, once again, the Cartesian worm of metaphysically separate self-consciousness, whose progeny are already wriggling vigorously around in Pascal's fragment on *le moi*. The lid can be replaced at least in part by recognizing that our whole dilemma with regard to what is 'internal' and what is 'external' to persons, our whole obsession with the supposedly radical difference of self-consciousness—all of that just *is* the can of worms of a particular philosophical tradition and of a particu-

---

[6] There is perhaps an important distinction to be made here between Strawson's interest in what constitutes an individual and my interest in the construction of personal identity. But I am not sure that the reductionist argument (finding the individual by cutting out all the things that are not specific to that one individual) works any better in his context than in mine.

[7] See the contribution of Sir Henry Harris to this volume. The argument that the genetic code is the only reliable measure of identity may be valid in forensic medicine, but it is in every other context disabling. Virtually everyone in the world has or uses a sense of identity without knowing anything about his or her genetic code, and Harris concedes that the possible outcomes from a given genetic code vary enormously according to circumstances of nurture.

lar intellectual culture. Although we cannot entirely escape from that tradition, since it has become an intrinsic part of the way we even begin to talk about such things, this move of containment may encourage us to look for alternative ways of speaking about identity.

This is another way of making the obvious but essential point that perceptions of identity are historically and culturally determined, and may vary very widely. Now this has an important consequence, which needs to be made explicit here: we have to be extremely careful and sensitive when dealing with perceptions foreign to the ones we take for granted. For example, one should ask: 'who is the "we" in that last sentence (not to mention quite a few other sentences in this essay)?' Since singular personal identity is nowadays such a highly prized achievement, who gets access to that privilege and who doesn't? Who is most allowed to *be* an individual? Shari Benstock and others, in a collection of essays on women's autobiographical writing called *The Private Self*, argue that the genre of autobiography has usually been defined by white males in terms of *their* conception of a free-range individualistic identity, ignoring the fact that women and non-whites have been consigned, relatively speaking, to a group identity, and may feel and express their identity primarily in that way (Benstock 1988: 10–33, 34–62, 273–4). My intention here is not to press one particular reading of this issue, but to show that all the critical problems—and, of course, all the critical interest—occur at the points where these different relational perceptions of identity intersect.

Finally, the modern and post-modern notions which one can broadly group under the label 'the deconstructed self' also take their place on this same cultural-historical axis. Pascal asks: is there an authentic self? So-called liberal humanists in the tradition of Montaigne and Locke have tended to give robustly positive answers: authenticity, for them, is located in an empirically constituted sense of self. Derrida, Foucault, and others have argued that this is a historically determinate construct which can be deconstructed without much difficulty. The self becomes an empty place crossed and recrossed by social, cultural, political, and above all linguistic traces; it is only the point where the co-ordinates happen to meet, precariously, before moving on. This view is an imaginatively powerful one, and it has perhaps been salutary in giving the gorged identities of liberal humanists a much-needed dose of salts (though some, of course, have refused to swallow the dose). But it is not the metaphysical 'answer' to the identity question, and it notoriously bears little relation to the practical sense of positioning and repositioning which ordinary individuals go through in order to find a name and a place that they can consider their own. As has recently been suggested,[8] it also risks cutting away the grounding which leads us to attribute the proper moral weight to the identity of others, and the rights that their claim to identity may entail. I want now to look at those more practical aspects of identity in terms of the question of narrative, of which the question of fiction is an unavoidable counterpart.

Identity, narrative, fiction

One may begin here with a crude but necessary working distinction between two kinds of identity narrative. There are non-fictional narratives (biographies), which claim to tell the story of real people and limit themselves in the main to verifiable circumstances; and there are fictional narratives, which make no such claim. It is important to know that some people really exist and that others are invented: the difference between Florence Nightingale and Jane Austen's Emma Woodhouse, between Bismarck and Captain Kirk, is a critical one, and we assign a different status to the narratives through which we find out who they are.

[8] See e.g. Johnson 1993, in which a number of leading theorists explore the apparent conflict (and possible conciliations) between the notion of a deconstructed self and the ethical imperatives of human rights.

However, it is also obvious that the stories of Florence Nightingale and Bismarck can be told in various ways, and that their identity may change quite radically as a result. Not, of course, their legal or biological identity: no story (other than a fictional one) can make it possible for Florence Nightingale to exchange identity cards or genetic codes or brains with Queen Victoria. But their moral and social identity, the kind of people they were, can be and have been defined differently by different narrative accounts; some of these will remain close to the available empirical information, others will embroider on it, invent dialogues and motives and secondary actions and events. We know what it means to say that some biographies of real people are close to fiction.

The name of Florence Nightingale already evokes this capacity of real people and real life-stories to become in some sense fictional, to be told in the mode of fiction (in this instance, as an exemplary moral story). A more problematic example is provided by a glossy hardback published recently under the title *Queen of Desire. Marilyn Monroe: A Fiction.* The author warns the reader that 'This is a work of fiction. The incidents as presented are wholly fictitious . . . The reader should not interpret any of the material as factual descriptions.' The blurb also claims that this is a 'compelling work of fiction', but then says that it 'comes nearer to the truth of the real Marilyn Monroe than any merely factual account ever could'. I have not read the book, and therefore cannot judge its merits or lack of them. I want first to bring out an inference that one can safely draw from those prefatory materials: namely, that in the late twentieth century a large number of readers know how to commute between fiction and reality. The book is fashionably postmodern, but not an avant-garde experiment: the play between reality and fiction, or truth and fiction, is clearly meant to be comprehensible—and saleable—to a relatively wide public.

Readers and audiences of other times and cultures have also known how to trade fictions off against a perceived reality; they have also been attracted by theatrical and other forms of impersonation. But in our own age, the saturation of images in the cinema and in other media has created that more intense kind of voyeuristic appropriation which is implied when one calls someone a 'media figure'. The 'real Marilyn Monroe' referred to in the blurb was already in part a fiction (beginning with her name). By this I mean that the fictionality through which she was exploited must have become part of her identity as she herself perceived it: she lived it. A collective manipulative desire imposed the identity *it* wanted on a pre-existing sense of self, creating pain and tension and alienation.

This, then, is a particularly strong version of the external-internal reciprocity I mentioned earlier. Stated in terms of narrative, one could say that a set of pre-fictional narratives attributable to the woman called Norma Jean Baker is invaded by the fictional narratives (film scripts, journalistic stories, biographies) associated with the name of Marilyn Monroe; we cannot know what it was like to be the real woman who had to accommodate that uncomfortable amalgam in a singular identity, but it is ethically and practically necessary to assume the existence of such a person.

This example brings out in a markedly sinister way the power of narrative to determine our sense of what identity is and where it is located. As Alasdair MacIntyre, Paul Ricœur, Peter Brooks, and others have remarked from their different points of view,[9] stories are being told endlessly by everyone, not only printed and televised stories which construct the

[9] MacIntyre 1985, ch. 15, esp. pp. 211–18; Ricœur 1992: 113–68; Brooks 1984, *passim*. Ricœur's study gives a more distinctively ethical turn to the narrative poetics elaborated in his three-volume work *Time and Narrative*; it provides the most comprehensive recent acount of the connection between narrative and identity, drawing on MacIntyre's work and indeed the whole philosophical tradition, Anglophone and Continental. For a briefer account, see Ricœur's lecture for the 1992 Oxford Amnesty series (Johnson 1993: 114–19). The recent interest of historians in the power of narrative to shape history should equally be mentioned here, since it raises questions germane to those of personal identity. The theme is, indeed, virtually a commonplace nowadays; all the more reason that it should feature prominently in at least one of the contributions to this volume. For a psychologist's perspective, see Bruner 1991.

identity of public figures, but personal and private stories. We all tell such stories, about ourselves and about each other, even though some of us no doubt do it more or better than others. Without the narrative structure they impose, our experience of the world and of ourselves would not be intelligible: it would only be a continuous given, in the way one supposes it must be for animals.

As in the instances I have already mentioned, we are not free, in these everyday narratives, to construct any identity at all (except in private fantasies of the Walter Mitty kind); but it is both possible and normal to give more than one account of the same segment of life and of the identity of the character or characters who figure in it. Not only may different people give different accounts of my behaviour and of what kind of person I am; I am also perfectly capable of telling my own story in different ways. The criterion of success in such cases is the power that a particular story will have to console or justify: human minds are particularly fertile in stories of self-justification, and one might note that the identity of others as narrative characters is likely to be manipulated in order to achieve this object. One might also want here to distinguish between different versions of a story which are compatible, and those which are incompatible: these last are particularly likely to cause trouble.

Such stories, then, are not strictly fictional, but their relation to the real world is not stable. They may indeed seem more fluid and ingeniously inventive than fiction, especially as they have to be continuously reassessed and updated to take account of shifting circumstances and new evidence. I may think that, like Lord Jim, I have committed a single lapse that has changed and even ruined my life; but three years later, I may decide that that reading was wrong and that the narrative had other possibilities I was not then aware of.[10] At all times, we make the hypothesis of a continuous personal identity and of an eventually determinate narrative embody-

[10] For a lucid and stimulating study of the question of narrative identity in *Lord Jim*, see Erdinast-Vulcan 1991: 34–47.

ing it; but we often find ourselves too much in the middle of things to make out clearly an ending which would stabilize the story and confirm its superiority to alternative versions (see Kermode 1973, chs. 2, 3, 5).

If this view is accepted, what is known generically as 'fiction' appears as a special variant of the inventive story-telling that goes on all the time. It is a special variant in that it is assigned to a separately marked out domain (symbolized by the shelves labelled 'fiction' in a bookshop or a library) where it is released from the constraint of rehearsing real bodies and real empirical circumstances; in return for this release, it is able to provide more determinate and complete models of narrative explanation. These may help us to tell better everyday stories, or show us what moral and social investments our stories may have. More centrally for what I am talking about here, they help us to try out our models of identity: it is not an accident, I think, that in the canons of fiction the plot of identity has always played such a prominent role, from the Frog Prince onwards.

This brings me to the topic of anagnorisis, which is Aristotle's term in the *Poetics* for the recognition of identity. Poetics is the study, among other things, of how narratives are made; if it is true that identity can only become intelligible through narrative, it follows that poetics is indispensable to the study of identity itself. I shall therefore now give a brief account of the fictional recognition plot, leading back to a restatement of the question of identity from that angle.[11]

Recognition

'Recognition' in this sense is patently an ancient and extremely widespread feature of fictional plots—a great deal more common in fiction, one might well think, than in life. The recognition scene is an extraordinary event, and its

---

[11] I have written about recognition at length in Cave 1988. The present essay is meant to place the topic in a new context and give it a new direction.

fictional representations are often perceived by readers and audiences as highly implausible, even absurd. Yet, from *Oedipus* and the *Odyssey* via medieval romance, Fielding and Dickens to Angela Carter's *Wise Children*, it has shown an extraordinary power to survive, to adapt itself to changes of culture and sensibility.

What all these fictions have in common is a severance, in time and also often in space: a body is lost, and later recovered for good or ill. Shakespeare's *The Winter's Tale* dramatizes that severance, the 'wide gap of time since first we were dissever'd'; and it does so in a form which makes wonderfully clear both its apparent implausibility and its overwhelming capacity to move the most incredulous member of the audience. It is true that, in more recent fictions (those written since the historical shift I mentioned earlier), severance of bodies has become less prominent; it is replaced by moral, social, and psychological disruptions, with consequent recognitions at those levels. I need only refer here randomly and nominally to the novels of Henry James, or to Proust's *A la recherche du temps perdu*, to illustrate a point that anyone familiar with the literary canon will easily grasp. Despite this change of emphasis, however, the trajectory of bodies—the startling things that may happen to them or that they may make happen—remains a crucial aspect of such plots. Critics and readers often claim to scorn mere material or physical recognition, but not much could go on without it.

Why then has the recognition plot survived, with all its risks of implausibility? I think one may answer this by saying that, like the counterfactual plots of science fiction, the recognition plot is a limit-case, which can have the value of testing the norms of identity itself and of the knowledge on which identity depends. The exceptional disruption of those norms exhibits the way in which they are constructed and the values which they imply. So, for example, recognitions are commonly reversals: Penelope recognizes a stranger to be her lost husband; Nora, in *A Doll's House*, recognizes the husband she has lived with for many years to be a stranger. In such ways, the recovery and identification of a body or of bodily continuity becomes the focus for notions of what, in addition to bodies, is essential to identity; of what values and commitments and possibilities of transgression identity carries; of what happens when our criteria for identification fail. The trajectory followed by Oedipus' body as it moves through ignorance to knowledge is fraught with moral, metaphysical, and also social implications. So is the unexpected re-emergence of the body of Magwitch which changes the life of Pip in *Great Expectations*.

There are of course also real-life versions of this story, however rarely they may occur: the problem of identifying a certain John Demjanjuk, for example, cannot be separated from the enormous ethical and historical questions which his case raises. If he was indeed wrongly identified as 'Ivan the Terrible' (himself a quasi-legendary figure), that was no doubt at least partly because the desire to identify that truly terrible and terrifying figure had become so intense. In these ways, the need or desire for recognition may—as in the instance of Marilyn Monroe—construct its own object, making it difficult to separate 'identity' from the values, desires, legal conventions, and so forth that are channelled through the recognition.

Impacted identity

This view of recognition plots as a dramatic convergence of different elements and perspectives may now be juxtaposed with certain moves made by recent philosophers who seek to show identity to be in some sense an amalgam, a singular concept with a composite character. This will take us to the very centre of the question we are considering.

The science fiction examples of Parfit and Williams focus on discontinuities that masquerade as continuities: is the teleported person the same as the one who entered the teleporter? If my brain is transplanted to another body, am I still the same person? These narrative experiments are attempts to explore a duality or complexity which has always worried philosophers concerned with the identity of persons. They suggest that it is very hard to make the complexity go away, and that, when we find it difficult to say where identity is located, the problem—as Bernard Williams elegantly puts it—is not so much in our words, but in our world.[12]

Strawson (1990: 101 ff.) is less obviously obsessed with lurid examples, but he does something essentially similar. He seeks to show that neither body nor mind is logically prior as the *locus* of identity; and that the only way out of the dilemma is to regard the concept of a person as 'primitive'. A person is not a duality in which one component is privileged, but an amalgam, awkward to analyse even though we seem to be able to get along with it reasonably well in everyday life. It is also an important part of Strawson's argument to say that our subjective sense of ourselves as individuals depends on our perception of individual others, and vice versa: this subject–object interdependence, or interpersonal perception of what it is to be an individual, again posits identity as an amalgam, joining what we are inclined to think of as essentially separate or different. One might be reminded here of recognition scenes in which individuals acquire a new sense of their identity not simply inwardly, by introspection, but in the glare of an interpersonal gaze: the endings of Shakespeare's comedies and romances again provide a rich set of models.

Alasdair MacIntyre (1985: 216–17) attempts to unravel what is essentially the same problem by reference to narrative. While discussing the importance of story-telling in broader terms, he turns to the more narrowly defined issue of personal identity, quoting Derek Parfit on the contrast between the all-or-nothing type of identity (is such-and-such a woman Florence Nightingale or Queen Victoria? Is the man here accused the concentration camp guard known as 'Ivan

---

[12] See above, p. 11.

the Terrible'?) and the more-or-less type of identity (was Queen Victoria at 60 the same woman as she was at 20? Am I the same person as I was last year, or last week, or this morning?). He argues that, as characters in enacted narratives, we have to be able to respond to the public and social demands of the first type, whatever the discontinuities and inconsistencies of the second. What may seem like two or more different persons inhabit a single bodily life and may be called to account morally, or may in other ways be obliged to accept an awkward and painful fusion of different narratives. Inversely, one may add, an individual with a strong sense of personal continuity invested in a particular set of memories may be forcibly removed from his or her environment and have to negotiate with alien kinds of identity. This is the predicament of exiles and of others who, like Odysseus, have undergone severance.

Another way of putting the same point is to say, again with MacIntyre (1985: 213), that the telling of identity-stories is necessarily a reciprocal activity: 'we are never more (and sometimes less) than the co-authors of our own narratives.' If he is right, the fact that I feature in other people's stories and they in mine is crucial to the continuous narrative construction of identity, but it also necessarily makes identity problematic, a site of many crossings over and displacements. One can see clearly here why the customary opposition between 'individual identity' and 'group identity' may be misleading. According to this kind of argument, it is *narrative* identity which is 'primitive' in the sense in which Strawson uses the word: identity is that which is contained in the narrative of the self, however incompatible its different elements and however uncomfortable their juxtaposition. And it is crucial that a bodily narrative (the 'all-or-nothing' type) constrains all the secondary narratives which may become associated with that bodily person.

Our personal identities may thus be, to a greater or lesser degree, painful, monstrous, impossible to comprehend except by means of strenuous narrative exegesis. Pascal (1963: 514;

fr. 130) says darkly that man is an incomprehensible monster because he is the conjunction of two violently different natures (it is perhaps better here not to tamper with Pascal's masculine pronoun). This is a theological statement, but it is also a philosophical and psychological perception.

Despite the differences in these accounts, the different things they join up and their various reasons for doing so, they all characterize identity as a puzzling amalgam, a *locus* of tension and unease. Identity is *impacted* (I use the word in the sense applicable to wisdom teeth). And it would seem that this painful place of crossing over is precisely the place displayed and probed by many, if not all, recognition plots. If recognition plots are implausible, it is primarily because they enact monstrous or marvellous or hilarious couplings: the coupling of a familiar body with an alien life history; the fusing of two apparently incompatible stories; the superimposition of a filial relation on a sexual one; the figure of the identical twin—a natural perspective that is, and is not. Hence, too, the association of recognition plots with enigmas and riddles and ambiguous sayings and oracles.

There is a final and crucial point which concerns the question of what, in addition to aesthetic and intellectual satisfaction, is at stake in our analysis of such representations. I am happy to accept Alasdair MacIntyre's argument that the everyday telling of identity-stories is fraught with ethical consequences. It would be hard to deny that it matters enormously how we tell our own and each other's stories. But I am concerned primarily here with those large, permanently made stories about imaginary people that we call literary fictions, and it is not my purpose to follow MacIntyre into the domain of Aristotelian ethics and the possibility of its revival. My appeal must be rather, once more, to Aristotelian poetics and *its* continuing value. The narrative structures displayed by poetics are not a mere form inhabited by moral and other themes, any more than personal identity is a particular body inhabited by a consciousness. They are rather a model of the processes by which we seek to comprehend that which borders on the incomprehensible. Fictional narratives present the awkward couplings of experience non-analytically, holistically, and—once again—in all their cultural and historical particularity. Poetics tries delicately to probe those couplings without reductively separating them.

Fictional identities

These points may now be illustrated by two examples from the nineteenth-century English novel; they are presented as case-studies of fictional identities, rather than as original contributions to the understanding of those particular texts.[13] I shall pay attention especially to the way in which the difficult balance between individual and social identity is structured through narrative, and to the problematic doublings or couplings which such fictional structures are capable of displaying.

Jane Austen's *Emma* is a classic comedy of errors in which mistakes about identity are central. Identity is defined here primarily through the social activity of matchmaking: the plot is structured by the errors that Emma makes in trying to marry people off who don't really match at all. Like the plots of other comedies, it is resolved when these errors are put right and the characters are settled with suitable partners. The errors, then, are mistakes about the moral and social identity of the characters concerned; the weddings at the end indicate that a stable and satisfactory set of identifications has been reached, marriage being the comic paradigm of a correct identification. So, for example, the uncertain—even dubious—moral identities of Frank Churchill and Jane Fairfax are cleared up in such a way as to identify them as socially viable and complementary, and the identification is publicly fixed and recognized by their marriage.

---

[13] For that reason, I shall make no reference to the critical literature on the two texts, except in one notorious case.

This suggests that the construction of identity in the world depicted by *Emma* is overwhelmingly 'external', directed towards the needs of the social group. Individual characters certainly manifest interiority, but the interest lies in the nego- tiations between that interiority and the pressure of the group, leading to its final absorption in a stable equilibrium perceived as happiness.

I shall focus here on the way in which these negotiations are structured by the plot, and in particular on the position within the plot as a whole of what one might call the 'Harriet Smith story'.

The narrative of Emma's attempts at matchmaking oper- ates at two levels. At the first level, it can be read as a kind of *Bildungsroman*: as Emma is gradually made to see her mis- takes, she becomes wiser and more down-to-earth and learns to act more responsibly; she achieves her true adult identity as the Emma who is worthy of Mr Knightley, a man of reason and of excellent social position (a man who is also suitably dismissive of fictions) (Austen 1990: 404). The structure of this plot is articulated by two scenes of recognition: the show- down between Emma and Mr Elton, quite early in the novel, in which it becomes clear that he loves Emma, not Harriet; and the more complex scene towards the end where the truth about Frank Churchill and Jane Fairfax emerges, throwing a decisive new light on the relations of the other characters. What is recognized in these scenes is, once again, the defini- tive moral and social identity of the characters concerned.

However, this reading marginalizes a strand in the plot which is in fact essential, although it is also marginalized by the emphasis and denouement of the novel itself, namely the question of Harriet's parentage. Harriet is the only character in the novel whose genealogical origin is hidden: she is known simply as an illegitimate child who has been sent to a school in Emma's village. Nourished on this open question, Emma's mistakes generate an alternative story, a romantic fiction of which Harriet Smith is intended to be the heroine: she jumps to the novelistic conclusion that Harriet is the daughter of a gentleman and so deserves to be matched with someone appropriate. It is only when all of the pairings (including Harriet's own) have already been achieved that Harriet gets *her* little recognition. The consequence is that Harriet's recognition comes as an anticlimax, exploding Emma's fictional inventions and confirming the status quo; in other words, it is exactly the reverse of the traditional dramatic anagnorisis. Harriet turns out to be the daughter of a well-off but otherwise obscure tradesman, and duly finds pastoral happiness with the modest but upright farmer Robert Martin.

The Harriet story is the most archaic strand in the recognition plot, the one most easy to recognize as the remnant of an old story: the mystery of the stray body, the foundling who may prove to have noble parents. Its relegation to a subordinate position in *Emma* is perfectly explicit. The reader is given ample indication that the foundling story is not only a romantic fiction, but also a childish and frivolous fiction: Jane Austen plays off her novel of banal everyday reality *against* such stories, against mysteries and riddles, gossip and story-telling.[14] In this way, *Emma* (the novel) does its level best to expel fictions, especially fictions of identity, and Emma (the character) explicitly grows away from her own fictional creation.

And yet, that old and discredited story—the story of the foundling—contains some troubling elements. One need only glance at the plot of *Emma* to show that the loss of one or both parents and the fostering of children are recurrent themes. Jane Fairfax, Miss Taylor (Emma's ex-governess), and Harriet all belong to a category of children who have lost their origins.[15] All of them are represented as having indi-

---

[14] Riddles, charades, and other games play a prominent part in the narrative. *Northanger Abbey* famously provides a less subtle variation on the clash between the everyday and the fictional: Catherine Morland, in the first chapter, regrets that there seems to be little chance in her environment of meeting a romantic foundling.

[15] Frank Churchill, as a fostered child, also belongs in part at least to this group, although, as a male, his future is somewhat less precarious. It is well known that Jane Austen's brother Edward was fostered with a family called the Knights, whose name is echoed in the Knightleys of *Emma*.

vidual bodies and character traits, which constitute a primary identity. But the realization of that identity depends crucially on their final placing in and by society. The vulnerability of Jane and Harriet is painfully exposed by the errors of the recognition plot; the reader is given plenty of signs of their inward distress.

Jane's distress, like Miss Taylor's before her, is eliminated by the intervention of comic good fortune; Harriet's, amazingly and inconsequentially, just goes away. Thanks to Emma's manipulations, she had fallen in love with Mr Knightley; she is sent to London to get over it; and she just *does* get over it. Emma can hardly believe her luck, and sees Harriet's change of heart as both 'unintelligible' and comically inconsequential.[16] It is all part of Harriet's general silliness, in other words her lack of a firm moral and emotional identity: just what one might expect of the illegitimate daughter of a tradesman. Yet the reader knows that Harriet did suffer, even if she is now supposed to be happy, and that Emma has got off lightly.

For this reason, one may argue that Jane Austen's precise model of the way in which identity is achieved in a given social microcosm remains at the end partially enigmatic. The impacting of the Harriet story on the story of Emma's progress towards marital identity and non-fictional happiness creates a discomfort, and the discomfort is most apparent at the very point where it is meant to be dispelled: that is to say, the point where Emma is let off the hook morally by the collapse of her own fantasies about Harriet's identity. What is the identity of the voice that is speaking at the narrative moment of Harriet's recognition?[17] Can Emma really be morally in the clear just because her erstwhile friend's emotions are so comically inconsistent? Whose voice is it that puts little Harriet back in her proper place? Is it Emma's?

[16] Austen 1990: 437–8; see also ibid. 432: 'She must laugh at such a close! Such an end of the doleful disappointment of five weeks back! Such a heart—such a Harriet!'
[17] Ibid. 438.

The narrator's? Is the reader supposed to perceive the inadequacy of such a response? It is not necessary, in the context of the argument I am proposing here, to resolve the problem: whichever way one takes it, the passage encapsulates in miniature the awkward relationship between two intertwined plots of identity, a legitimate one and an illegitimate one.

Emma takes place in a small and closed world. With *Daniel Deronda*, we have the explicit opening of such a world on to a wider horizon in which identity becomes problematic in a very different sense. Thus Gwendolen Harleth, who seems in the earlier part of the novel to be a wilfully self-reliant character and who chooses, however disastrously, her public and social identity as the wife of Grandcourt, is finally displaced into a kind of anonymity:

The world seemed getting larger round poor Gwendolen, and she more solitary and helpless in the midst . . . That was the sort of crisis which was at this moment beginning in Gwendolen's small life: she was for the first time . . . being dislodged from her supremacy in her own world, and getting a sense that her horizon was but a dipping onward of an existence with which her own was revolving. (Eliot 1988: 688–9)

It is as if George Eliot had taken Emma out of her china teacup circle, made her pay in full for her errors by being herself mismatched, and then projected her out into a world made fraught by issues such as the Jewish claim to a national home.

In order to produce this ethical explosion, two recognition plots (each complex enough in its own right) have to collide: the personal recognition plot in which Gwendolen Harleth eventually discovers that the English gentleman she has married is a monster, and Daniel Deronda's endlessly ramifying recognition of an ethnic and historical identity.

The conventional response to this second plot is that it is a bad mistake on George Eliot's part: implausible, tasteless, and mawkish, it stages Jews who are caricatural both in their crudely commercial manners and in their visionary obsessions. There are two famous instances of this response: Henry

James's (1876) critical dialogue, in which uppercrust characters discuss the defects of Eliot's novel; and Leavis's (1948:
122) contention that, if all the Jewish bits were excised,
Daniel Deronda would become worthy of the great tradition
of the English novel.

The first reply to such judgements is that Jewish identity is
not an essence, a timeless property shared by all authentic
Jews. Therefore it is entirely understandable historically that,
in George Eliot's novel, Jewishness is identified by and
against English country-house manners: that is to say, by and
against an Englishness which is itself abrasively identified in
the process. It is also necessary to accept that such an identification must fall within the limits of what was possible for an
unusually sympathetic and sensitive observer at that time;
one may note that the novel earned applause from many
Jewish sources, in its own day and later.

To chart responses in which social and personal embarrass-
ment plays such a central role, George Eliot has to embarrass
the reader: she has to break the mould of the country-house
novel, bring something as it were unmentionable into it. The
hinge on which this confrontation turns is the blankness of
Deronda's identity, a space that remains open to the workings of chance; it is perhaps not surprising that this blankness has irritated critics of the novel no less than its Jewish
ramifications.

We have space here for only one illustration, taken from a
relatively early stage in the plot. Deronda has been brought
up in the country-house world as an English gentleman; he
believes that his 'uncle' is really his father (in fact, he is
neither), and this in turn entails a sense of exclusion from the
paternal heritage. He saves the life of a young Jewish woman
called Mirah, and this new element in his life—a personal
contact with Jewishness—disturbs him. He goes to Germany
and visits the synagogue in Frankfurt. Into this part of the
narrative is intercalated a reflection on his lack of some clear
purpose which would define him in relation to the social
world:

But how and whence was the needed event to come?—the influence that would justify partiality, and make him what he longed to be yet was unable to make himself—an organic part of social life, instead of roaming in it like a yearning disembodied spirit, stirred with a vague social passion, but without fixed local habitation to render fellowship real? (Eliot 1988: 308)

A sense of deficient identity is represented here by a metaphor of disembodiment, as if existing in the social world were coterminous with having a body, and as if having that social body were necessary in order to fulfil the requirement of determinate identity.

A page later, what one might call a Pascalian glance falls on Deronda. In the synagogue, an old Jew looks at him closely, puts his hand on his arm, and asks him about his parentage, his mother's family and maiden name. Upset by this liberty (and by his consciousness of not knowing the answer), Deronda only replies coldly 'I am an Englishman' and turns away (ibid. 311). He will need to go through many other recognitions—Mordecai's, for example, in the following chapter, and eventually his mother's—before he is ready to accept his genealogical identity and its wide-ranging ethical and social implications. And by that time he will precisely not be a well-rounded character in the small world of country-house fiction, but a personification of larger issues—'world-historical' issues, to use a term which is close to George Eliot's way of conceiving such things.

In this way, Daniel Deronda has to be, in his singular bodily identity, both an English gentleman and a Jew; not an Englishman who has Jewish origins which he has successfully concealed, but one who takes on the full responsibility of his Jewish genealogy. He has to live out that seemingly impossible identity which is a fusion of, say, Grandcourt and Mordecai. So, too, does the novel: the discomfort of generations of readers is traceable, I think, to that awkward doubling, to Deronda's impacted identity and its structural consequences. Like Gwendolen, the reader has to learn, painfully, how to emerge out of the familiar novelistic framework of which she was the protagonist; how to move through fiction into history.

It is not difficult, in fact, to show that *Daniel Deronda* is *about* history and how it is embedded in the personal and the particular, in questions of identity. For the novel counterpoints the itinerary of Deronda's personal discovery of identity with events on the European stage, recording not only the Jewish claim to a national home but also the Prussian victories of the 1860s. That must already have seemed quite an ambitious project when the novel first appeared. For us, however, the trajectory the novel begins to describe—the trajectory of Deronda and Mirah's bodies as they leave for Palestine—has gone incalculably further, determining the very character of twentieth-century experience and raising the problem which most urgently faces the world now, whether one is thinking of the Palestinian question, of the former Jugoslavia, or of Quebec: the unmanageable explosion of the politics of identity. That later trajectory makes it impossible for us not to attribute the greatest historical and moral seriousness to the poetics of *Daniel Deronda*.

We thus return to the notion of a poetics bound up, in several senses, with history; a poetics which is itself an identifying structure. What it identifies in a given fictional narrative is primarily a mode of experience in its relative distance from our own; but that identification can in its turn provide a coordinate which may help us to locate where our own values lie, how they are constructed and how they may warp or fall apart or just prove inadequate. Poetics is in this sense inseparable from the many-sided question of identity, and shares with law, philosophy, anthropology, and history the responsibility of attempting to understand that question.

The strength of poetics does not lie in its generalizing power, in its capacity to produce an invariant model transcending all particulars. It lies rather in its ability to identify the distinctive individual properties of fictional narratives, and consequently their infinitely varied embodiment of practical human experience.

I use the word 'embodiment' here in its literal sense. The fictional plots of identity demonstrate how much may depend on the contingent recovery of a body, and how that recovery may be, must be, a focus of the social and ethical narratives without which identity is an empty space filled only with an insatiable psychic hunger. It follows that the study of fictional identities is not the pretext for an escape from responsibility into formalism or aesthetic relativism, but the reverse: namely, the point from which the practice of reading may lead back into the practice of living.

6

The Formation of National Identity

ANTHONY D. SMITH

There is nothing peculiarly modern about the problem of identity. It is almost as old as recorded history. Certainly, the Bible contains many instances of concern with ethnic and social identity, individual and collective. Jacob's simulation of his brother Esau's identity, Ruth's determination to exchange her Moabite for an Israelite identity and Jonah's assertion of his Hebrew identity despite his refusal to accept his prophetic mission, are among the better-known examples. Ancient Greek mythology, too, reveals a strong interest in problems of social identity; Ion, Theseus, and, in more tragic vein, Orestes all suffer from self-doubt or internal conflicts. Perhaps the most celebrated of these cases was Oedipus, who in the course of Sophocles' play, runs through several would-be identities, only to stand revealed as a parricide, husband of his mother, brother of his sons and daughters, and a Theban after all.

That last identity, membership of the *polis* from which Oedipus was so soon to be exiled, was all-important for ancient Greeks, as was the community for Israelites and other ancient peoples. To be sundered from it, to be blotted out from the congregation in the biblical phrase, was to lose one's social identity and become an outcast. Just as to be ignorant of one's lineage, or to be of the wrong or a divided lineage, was to have no identity, or one that was inadmissible.

These problems, and they have reappeared in all epochs, reveal two concerns. One is summed up in the familiar modern question, *Who* am I?; the other in that even more pressing problem, *What* am I? The first is generally answered by an assertion of continuity through genealogy and residence, the second by an assertion of distinctiveness through culture and community. Most people feel they can provide a satisfactory answer to the first question by pointing to their lineage, family status, and place of birth or residence. To answer the second question, however, they have to reveal their membership of and adherence to particular cultures and distinctive communities. For individuals, of course, the two questions are intertwined; but here I shall be concentrating mainly on the second question, the 'what' identity, since my concern is with *national identity*.

The elements of collective cultural identities

Identity operates on two levels, the individual and the collective. The two levels are often confused in discussions of ethnic and national identity. I shall argue that, while collective identities are composed of individual members, they are not reducible to an aggregate of individuals sharing a particular cultural trait. Similarly, from a description of the elements composing a collective cultural identity one cannot read off the probable actions or dispositions of individual members, only the kinds of contexts and constraints within which they operate. Hence the need to keep the two levels of identity, individual and collective, separate (Scheuch 1966).

My concern here is with collective cultural identities. Human beings have a wide variety of possible collective affiliations—economic and occupational groups, leisure and welfare associations, age and gender categories, territorial and political organizations, as well as families and cultural communities. With all of these individuals can simultaneously identify, moving with relative ease from one to the other, as circumstances demand. We may be wives or husbands, manual workers, members of a religious community, ethnic group, regional association, or whatever, each of which may become relevant in certain situations and for certain purposes. As a result, we have multiple identities, ranging from the most intimate family circle to the widest, the human species (Okamura 1981).

Certain varieties of these multiple identities have always exerted a special power. These are the specifically cultural types of collective identities. Examples of such collective cultural identities include castes, ethnic communities, religious denominations, and nations. Other collective identities, such as classes, regions, and gender groups, may also have cultural dimensions, but they function mainly as interest groups, answering to particular collective needs. They have often been overshadowed in history by more intense and pervasive cultural identities, because the basic cultural elements from which these communities have been forged are more tenacious and binding than the shared needs and interests that characterize other kinds of collective identity.[1]

These basic cultural elements—symbols, values, memories, myths, and traditions—embody certain recurrent dimensions of cultural community and identity. The most important of these are:

1. a sense of stability, and rootedness, of the particular cultural unit of population;
2. a sense of difference, of distinctiveness and separateness, of that cultural unit;
3. a sense of continuity with previous generations of the cultural unit, through memories, myths, and traditions;
4. a sense of destiny and mission, of shared hopes and aspirations, of that culture-community.

These dimensions of community and identity are embodied in various cultural elements—the symbols, values, myths, memories, and traditions of the community, and the artefacts that express them. Memories of past sacrifices, of victories

[1] For such collective cultural identities as primordial 'givens', see Geertz 1963 and Stack 1986, Introduction, a view challenged by Bell 1975 and Brass 1979.

and defeats, of ancient deeds of heroism—as Renan suggested—express our sense of continuity with previous generations. Traditions—including customs, law codes, genealogies, and rituals—impart a sense of stability and rootedness to the community. Symbols such as flags, emblems, anthems, costume, special foods, and sacred objects, give expression to our sense of difference and distinctiveness of the community. Values of collective courage, honour, wisdom, compassion, and justice confer a sense of mission and dignity on the community; while myths of origins, liberation, the golden age, and chosenness link the sacred past to a sense of collective destiny. Each of these elements articulates a vital dimension of the culture-community (Renan 1882; A. D. Smith 1984*a*).

It is important to stress that collective cultural communities and identities do not constitute some fixed and constant quantity of traits, or an unchanging underlying essence. They too are subject to the unceasing flux of social life, so that we can in principle trace their origins, growth, and decay, as with any other kind of collective identity and community. But the rhythms of specifically cultural collective identities are generally slower and longer-lasting than those of other types of identity, a fact of considerable significance for the analysis of ethnic survival over the *longue durée*.[2]

Ethnic and national identities

The broadest subtype of collective cultural identities is the *ethnie*, or ethnic community. Ethnies are characterized by a sense of origin, a sense of distinctiveness and a sense of place. They are more than mere categories; they are communities. An ethnic category, by contrast, is a population that others deem to constitute a historic group on the basis of one or more shared cultural characteristics; but the ethnic category

---

[2] On 'modernism' and 'perennialism', see A. D. Smith 1988.

lacks the other elements of an ethnie. Its members are un-aware of their historic relationship; they lack a myth of com-mon ancestry. They also have little or no sense of community. Like the pre-modern Slovaks or Ewe, they may live in adja-cent hamlets or valleys, but feel little sense of kinship (Brock 1976; Welch 1966).

An ethnie, by contrast, is a definite historic culture-com-munity, some of whose members share a sense of solidarity. The main features of an ethnie are:

1. a collective name, which symbolizes the uniqueness of the community and demarcates it from others;
2. a myth of common origins, which relates all the mem-bers to a common ancestor, birthplace, and foundation;
3. a shared ethno-history, that is, the shared memories of successive generations of a culture-community;
4. one or more common cultural characteristics which can serve to demarcate members from non-members, such as colour, language, customs, religion, and institutions;
5. an association with a historic territory, or homeland, even where most of the community no longer resides in it;
6. a sense of solidarity on the part of at least a significant segment of the culture-community.

Consequently, we can define the ethnie as a named culture-community whose members have a myth of common origins, shared memories and cultural characteristics, a link with a homeland and a measure of solidarity (see Schermerhorn 1970; Horowitz 1985, ch. 2; A. D. Smith 1986*a*, ch. 2).

There are three main kinds of ethnic community in the historical record: ethno-linguistic, ethno-religious, and ethno-political. Ethno-linguistic communities are perhaps the most common type, certainly in Europe. Here members share a common vernacular code and literature, which de-fines the cultural characteristics which set the community off from its neighbours. These form the essential 'border guards' of ethnicity, although other elements are also operative. In communities like Quebec, Brittany, Catalonia, and Kurdistan language is the most salient and vital element in the definition of ethnicity and the mobilization of ethnic sentiments (Krejci 1979; Fishman 1980).

Ethno-religious community has also been very common. In antiquity and the early Middle Ages, religious cleavages figured alongside linguistic, as the most important cultural characteristics demarcating ethnic communities. The best-known cases have been the Armenians and Jews, but other ethnies like the Serbs, Irish, and Sikhs have been defined, and have defined themselves, primarily in terms of religious beliefs, practices, and symbols. Ethno-religious communities remain widespread and vital to this day (Atiyah 1968; Armstrong 1982, chs. 3, 7).

Finally, ethno-political communities—communities that have defined themselves, and been defined, by historical memories and political traditions—have also been prominent in several periods. Ancient Egypt stands as the prototype. Other examples include republican Rome and its Latin League, Sassanid Persia, and the Swiss Confederation. In each of these cases, a political myth of foundation and historical memories have welded together disparate but related groups into an 'ethnic state'. Even after the dissolution of the polity, the memory of former statehood plays a vital role in the definition and expression of ethnicity (see Nairn 1977, ch. 5; Krejci and Velimsky 1981).

The world today is filled with various kinds of ethnic community, linguistic, religious, and political, or combinations of these. Many of these communities lay claim to being nations and seek states of their own. Can we admit their claim? Is there a Basque or Kurdish national identity, as opposed to an ethnic one? Is there any difference between ethnic and national identity?

Some scholars regard nations simply as self-aware ethnic groups, or treat the two terms as synonyms. That they are related to each other, as the terminology of the Greek *ethnos* and the Latin *natio* suggests, is clear. But, ethnies and nations are not identical, nor are they distinguishable simply by the degree of their members' self-awareness (Hertz 1944; Zernatto 1944; Connor 1978).

Nations and national identities are best regarded as a special subvariety and development of ethnies and ethnic identities. Nations share with ethnies their cultural features such as historical memories, ancestry myths, and shared cultural traits; but they are distinguishable from ethnies by their possession of other components and processes. These include:

1. a definite historic territory or homeland (and not just an association with it),
2. a common economy, with territorial mobility throughout,
3. a shared public, mass education-based culture,
4. and common legal rights and duties for all members.

This allows us to define the nation as a named community occupying a recognized homeland and possessing shared myths and memories, a mass public culture, a common economy and uniform legal rights and duties (A. D. Smith 1991, ch. 1).[3]

On this view, national identity represents a composite and multidimensional amalgam of processes, which develop in unequal rhythms. These include growing territorialization, the growth of a mass public culture, economic centralization, and legal standardization—as well as the cultivation of historical myths and memories drawn from earlier ethnies. Like ethnic identity, national identity is no fixed quantity of elements, no static essence, but an often fluid set of processes and dimensions which over time create the sense of a national community or nation. National identity differs from ethnicity, however, in giving more weight to territorial, economic, and legal-political processes. At the same time, the nation needs

[3] This is a largely 'objectivist' and 'ethnicist' definition (as opposed to 'subjectivist' and 'statist'), though it allows for the role of 'subjective elements' like myths, memories, and symbols. There is a vast literature on definitions of 'nation' and 'nationalism'; see Rustow 1967, ch. 1; Connor 1978; A. D. Smith 1983, ch. 7.

to be distinguished from the state. Whereas the state is best viewed as a set of public, autonomous institutions with a legitimate monopoly of coercion and extraction in a given territory, the nation constitutes a territorial community of shared history, culture, and legal rights (see Tilly 1975, Introduction; Tivey 1980, Introduction).

The ethnic bases of national identities

In general terms, the formation of national identity can be traced through the often uneven development of the processes that constitute this particular kind of community. But it must also be related to the dominant ethnie which constitutes the basic building block of the nation-to-be, and to the different kinds of ethnic community which form the starting-points of these developments. Many of today's nations, as our definitions indicate, have been formed on the basis of a 'core ethnie', which acted as the original unit and prime mover of that polity.[4]

We need to distinguish at the outset between this 'core ethnie', the state, and the nation. All three are historically, as well as conceptually, distinct. In England, for example, an Anglo-Saxon ethnie was gradually formed from the fifth century onwards; but it was one which was until the tenth century divided into several kingdoms—Kent, Wessex, Mercia, etc. In the absence of a mass, public culture, demarcated territory, unified economy and standardized legal rights, we cannot yet speak of an Anglo-Saxon, or English, nation. Even the unification of these kingdoms by Anglo-Saxon and Danish rulers into a single state only hastened some of the processes of forming a nation—territorial unification and legal standardization, for example—before the Norman

[4] Though in part an empirical tautology, the relationship between ethnie and nation suggested here is, I believe, an illuminating one, exactly because it highlights those elements that are peculiar to the concept of the nation, over and above the elements shared with ethnies.

Conquest added complex new social and cultural elements (see L. Smith 1984; Howe 1989).

The process of forging an English nation was resumed in the thirteenth century and encouraged by the Anglo-Scottish and Anglo-French Wars. This was largely a result of the consolidation of an English state by an aristocratic ethnie. Even then, only the upper strata could participate in that incipient national community. It took the Reformation and the Puritan ideology of chosenness to diffuse a sense of common nationality to the middle classes; and the industrial and democratic revolutions of the nineteenth century to incorporate the majority of the population, including women, into the nation. It is a process which continues today, as new immigrants seek entry into an English culture and a British political community (Kohn 1940; Corrigan and Sayer 1985; Samuel 1989).

In this example, state and nation are distinguished not merely from each other, but also from the ethnie which forms their basis. Whereas the state is a political-legal organization, ethnies and nations are social and cultural communities. Nations differ from the more numerous ethnies in also defining themselves and being defined as territorial communities with a mass public culture and common laws for all members.

So the process of turning an ethnie into a nation is one that is associated with the politicization of culture, the delimitation of space and the standardization of social life. These are all concomitants of complex forms of society (as Herbert Spencer would have termed it), but they are also linked to more specific modern developments. While we can find instances of the process of ethnies-turning-into-nations even in antiquity—for example, the Jews in the Second Temple era—this phenomenon is relatively rare until the late medieval period; whereas it becomes common as we move into the modern era (Neusner 1981; Grosby 1991).

In pre-modern periods, we sometimes encounter the formation of 'ethnic states', states that are dominated by and operated on behalf of particular ethnies. The most familiar case is probably ancient Egypt, whose compact settlement on the banks of the Nile and protection by deserts imbued the native inhabitants of 'the land' with a clear sense of cultural difference from, and superiority to, others like the Asiatic Hyksos. But economic localism, the different kinds of education open to different classes, and their different legal rights and duties, prevented the transition to any idea of a mass nation with natural and/or historic boundaries and a single, public culture and legal order. The same was true of other ethnic states in antiquity, such as the Elamites, Hittites, Philistines, and Achaemenid Persians, as well as several barbarian *regna* of early medieval Europe— Franks, Lombards, Visigoths, and, as we saw, Anglo-Saxon England—not to mention Tokugawa Japan. (See Trigger *et al.* 1983; Wiseman 1973; Tipton 1972; Reynolds 1984, ch. 8; Lehmann 1982.)

Yet, in some cases, the presence and centrality of a 'core ethnie' did form the basis for the development of the nation. This was not simply a matter of the accidents of geography and later state formation. The vicissitudes of the Italian case demonstrate that there is no simple linear descent from an earlier ethnic state, in this case the Lombard kingdom, to the modern Italian nation, even if that myth could be revived in the ideology of the present-day Lombard League. What also has to be kept alive in popular consciousness is the memory and symbolism of historical distinctiveness or statehood.

This is not just another formulation of Hegel's theory of the 'history-less peoples'. For Hegel, only those peoples who had been able to forge states in the past would be likely to do so again in the future and thereby become full nations. This is clearly a restrictive, and a politically partial, criterion. What I am arguing instead, is that the presence or absence of a 'core ethnie', with or without an ethnic state, is relevant only if there is also a vivid sense of ethno-history which has been nourished in the popular consciousness, and which forms part of a popular heritage and collective memory (Rosdolsky 1964).

'Ethno-history' denotes, not the disinterested enquiries of professional historians into ethnic pasts, but the highly selective myths and memories of the members of a given ethnic community or nation. This ethnic past is usually seen as a single tradition, though one often interwoven with specific local traditions. For example, Mongols till today combine their local clan traditions with vivid memories of Ghenghis Khan and the vast ethnic state which he forged on the plains of Central Asia in the thirteenth century. And the Amhara and Tigre of Ethiopia still recall their pre-European ethnic kingdoms and civilizations.

Now the sense of ethno-history is unevenly distributed across the globe. In some cases, there are rich and well-documented memories of a past stretching back centuries, and even millennia. Examples of this spring readily to mind: the ethno-history of Greeks, Armenians, Jews, Persians, and Chinese can trace their collective past, and their historic culture-community, back into antiquity, irrespective of the probability that in most cases the demographic composition, as well as the cultural content, of the identified community has radically changed. The well-known disputes about the descent of modern Greeks from the ancient Greeks, which followed Fallmerayer's thesis about the effects of the Slav and Albanian invasions of Greece in the seventh century on the composition and culture of the area, are a case in point. But, on another level, the historicity of ethnic assertions is irrelevant. The passionate belief of most modern Greeks in their demographic and cultural kinship with their ancient forbears, feeds and shapes modern Greek self-understanding as no amount of disinterested historical enquiry could ever do (Carras 1983; Just 1989; Kitromilides 1989).[5]

In general, the sheer richness and diversity of historical sources is often a powerful spur to the sense of ethnic identity today, as it has been in the past. In other cases, an ethnic past

[5] Hence the efforts by modern scholars like Kedourie (1960) and Hobsbawm (1990) to 'debunk' the false historical assertions of nationalists are, from a sociological point of view, beside the point.

is less well documented. Intellectuals have to reconstruct from patchy evidence some notions about a collective past they fervently desire to embrace and display. Heroes are shadowy figures, battles dimly recalled, and there is confusion over the origins and early history of the community. Even a sense of community may be weak and confined to small circles at the centre. For pre-modern Slovaks or Yoruba before the advent of European scholars and missionaries, there were only the haziest ideas about the ancestral tie that linked them, only the vaguest historical memories of past glories or political action, and only very limited communication between their valleys, villages, clans, and tribes. Ethno-history had to be recovered from the mists of time, so that communal dignity could be restored, even if this meant 'reconstructing', and in some cases 'inventing', the ethnic past (Brock 1976; Peel 1989).

The uneven distribution of ethno-history is closely linked to the development of an effective myth of ethnic election. This is much more than a sense of the centrality and rightness of 'our' community, or the plain ethnocentrism that judges other communities by the yardstick of one's own. A myth of ethnic election asserts that the chosen people has certain privileges because it performs specified duties to the deity, to itself and to others. It must accept a moral and ritual code of conduct and fulfil its obligations, if it is to retain its chosen position in the cosmic dispensation. The first clear example of such a myth occurs in the Pentateuch, which declares the Israelites to be a 'holy nation' and a people of priests. In their wake, several ethnies, from the Armenians, the 'first Christian nation', to the Persians, Russians, Byzantine Greeks, French, English, Welsh, Irish, and Americans have fortified themselves through many tribulations with the invincible belief in their own God-given mission and election. Such myths have played an important role in extending the life-span of smaller and weaker ethnies whom one might otherwise have expected to succumb and be absorbed by the larger populations that surrounded them. They have often helped to redress the balance of power between different ethnies, and have proved to be invaluable inner resources when it came to staking out national claims in an often hostile international environment (Tudor 1972; A. D. Smith 1992).

Stages of nation formation

The presence or absence of ethnic ties in an area or population; the rise of ethnic cores and peripheries; the preservation of a fund of ethno-historical memories; and the cultivation of myths of ethnic election: these are some of the ethnic bases for the subsequent formation of nations. But how did a more political and territorial concept of the nation develop from these ethnic origins? Can we discern any stages, patterns, or routes in the formation of nations?

As a rough guide, we can distinguish a series of stages in the formation of nations which, though no evolutionary law, holds, with certain variations, for the great majority of nations.

1. The first stage is that of ethnic origins, the coalescence of clans and tribes, settlements and villages, into wider cultural and political networks. This period is associated with myths of ancestry, migration, and liberation; and above all with foundation myths. Among the best known are the Roman foundation myths of Romulus and Remus, and of Trojan Aeneas' wanderings and battles in Italy; and the Israelite myths of the Patriarchs, enslavement in Egypt, the Exodus and the Covenant on Mount Sinai, under Moses' leadership. Most European ethnies boast similar myths of ancestry, migration, and foundation such as the Saxon migration under Hengist and Horsa, Clovis and the Frankish conquest, the Piast dynasty in Poland, and the Varangian origins of Rus, and make similar claims to classical or biblical lineage (Tudor 1972; Reynolds 1983; A. D. Smith 1984a).

2. This is succeeded by a period of ethnic consolidation, recalled as a 'golden age' by later generations. It is often

associated with the flowering of ethnic culture, the performance of military exploits, and the presence of sages, saints,
and heroes. The Irish looked back to the period just before
and after St Patrick as their golden age, when Irish art and
poetry, religion, and scholarship flourished. Similarly, the
post-Vedic era of classical city-states, the period of Buddha,
the epics and Upanishads, was later seen as a great and
glorious Indian religious civilization. Later generations of
Jews saw in the kingdom of David and Solomon a golden
age of their people; just as later Romans looked back to the
stern republican virtues of the age of Scipio and Cato as
their moral standard (Hutchinson 1987; McCulley 1966;
Eisenstein-Barzilay 1959; Balsdon 1979).

3. There follows a third period, of development and division, often seen as decline. The old order hardens around the
upper classes, the community ossifies and decays and is sometimes conquered and exiled, as with the Irish and Jews. In
England, later generations yearned for the presumed liberties of the Anglo-Saxon era, contrasting them with the
'Norman Yoke' that followed the Conquest. In France, the
ancien regime with its aristocratic privileges inspired a similar
desire for a simpler, nobler past; while many a Slavophile
under the later Tsars longed for the pre-Petrine simplicities
of 'Old Russia' (MacDougall 1982; Barzun 1932; Thaden
1964).

4. This is where nationalism, the desire to 'reawaken' and
'regenerate' the community, finds fertile soil. Nationalist
revolutions reconstruct the past as that of the pre-existent
nation, to be roused from its long sleep and cleansed of alien
disfigurements. But the nationalist myth represents a break
with the past, even as it recasts it. Firmly tied to a vision of the
future, it seeks to impart a sense of destiny and mission to the
people. Its use of the past is therefore selective, singling out
foundation myths and golden ages, and omitting unworthy
episodes and embarrassing interpretations. In some cases,
nationalists will reconstruct a sketchy past or even invent
episodes. A telling example was the publication of the

Finnish *Kalevala* in 1835 by Elias Lonnrot. He collected the ballads of Karelian peasants to compose the Finnish epic, which soon came to be regarded as a poetic portrayal of ancient Finland, a Northern equivalent of the Homeric epics, with which the Finnish intelligentsia was able to mobilize the people against an oppressive Russian regime (Branch 1985).

5. Finally, there is the period of the modern nation. Here the emphasis falls upon the provision of a national constitution, the institution of a regular political system, the development of a modern economy and legal order, and the emancipation and provision of social welfare for all classes and for women. Only then can we begin to speak of a fully-fledged 'mass nation', and of the normalization of its nationalism as an accepted feature of an international system (Smith 1979; Connor 1990).

We can briefly illustrate these five stages in the development of the Swiss nation. Memories of the migrations of the Alemannic tribes were preserved in the early Swiss chronicles, as were the much later attempts by the Habsburgs to take away cantonal and urban rights. The ensuing struggle was dramatized in the myth of political foundation—the Oath of the Rütli of 1291 and the exploits of William Tell. In the second stage, the Swiss *Eidgenossenschaft* was established through a series of victories over the Habsburg forces, at Morgarten (1315), Sempach (1386), and Näfels (1388), and the accession of the free cities of Berne, Lucerne, and Zurich. Despite internal divisions, this was a period of expansion and heroism culminating in the triumph over Burgundy at Grandson and Moret (1476) (Im Hof 1991).

The sixteenth century began a period of consolidation and decline. After the divisions of Zwingli's Reformation and the accession of Geneva and other French-speaking cities, the Old Confederation gradually ossified as a closed urban patriciate which crushed some serious peasant revolts, confined political rights to a small ruling class and kept a number of cantons in a dependent state. The fourth stage opened with the movement of enlightenment and regeneration among intellectuals like Bodmer, Lavater, and Füssli, and in 1798 French Revolutionary troops overthrew the ruling Bernese patriciate and set up the Helvetic Republic. A new secular Swiss national sentiment spread by progressive intelligentsia triumphed in the religious war of 1847. Finally, a modern Swiss nation was inaugurated by the 1848 Constitution and the laws of 1874, through a modern, secular federal state, a system of public education, and gradual enfranchisement of all classes (Kohn 1957; Fahrni 1983).

Three patterns of formation of nations

Within this general schema of national formation, there are significant variations in the routes by which nations have emerged. The most important is the type of ethnic base of the nation-to-be, that is, whether it was formed on the basis of a 'lateral' or 'vertical' ethnie.

In the 'lateral' or aristocratic type of ethnie, the ethnic culture is largely confined to the upper classes of the community. The mass of the peasantry and the outlying areas lie outside that culture and community. Even where they are nominally of the same ethno-linguistic, ethno-religious, or ethno-political community, the peasants and artisans often have a variety of cultures. 'Lateral' communities have far-flung and ragged boundaries, with much intermarriage between upper strata members of different ethnies. Examples of this type of ethnie include the Hittites and ancient Persian aristocracy, the Hungarian knights, and the Catalan nobility.

In contrast, 'vertical' or demotic ethnies are culturally concentrated and compact. A single ethnic culture tends to permeate all strata and areas of the community, and barriers to marriage with outsiders are higher. Despite their conflicts, the different classes share in the common fund of symbols, memories, myths, and traditions. Examples of the demotic type are ethno-religious communities like the Jews,

Orthodox Greeks and Armenians, Druse, Maronites, Sikhs, and Catholic Irish, as well as ethno-political city-state communities like ancient Sumer, Phoenicia, and Greece, where a common religion and pantheon, dialects, and institutions, along with protracted wars against outsiders, bred a sense of ethnic unity among culturally similar populations (A. D. Smith 1986*a*, ch. 4).

The 'vertical' and 'lateral' types include the majority of ethnies. But a third type has become more important in the modern world: the 'emigrant-colonist' ethnie. Examples include the early United States, British Canada, Australia, South Africa, and Argentina. Here a part of an older ethnic community emigrates overseas to form a new ethnie, and then admits or is deluged with new immigrants of other old ethnies. The result is a mixed political community, one based initially on a core, and perhaps still strategic, ethnic group, but now composed of many migrant part-ethnies as well (Seton-Watson 1977, ch. 5).

These socio-political types provide the main ethnic bases for processes of nation formation. But what are the causal processes that shape their transformation into nations?

Broadly speaking, we must distinguish between two routes of nation formation. The first proceeds through bureaucratic incorporation consequent on an economic and administrative revolution and based on a 'lateral' or aristocratic ethnie; the second through a cultural revolution, vernacular mobilization and the politicization of culture, which transform 'vertical' or demotic ethnies into nations. Some examples may help to clarify my meaning.

Let me start with familiar terrain, France. The Frankish conquerors of the sixth century are best characterized as a 'lateral' or aristocratic ethnie, ruling over a culturally different Romano-Gallic population. After the collapse of the Carolingian empire, and a long interregnum, the Frankish Capetians managed by stages to consolidate a strong state around the Île de France, with the help of the Church, notably the archbishops of Rheims. By the thirteenth century they had managed to incorporate some professional and middle strata and outlying areas such as Normandy and Languedoc; and after another period of weakness, the process was accelerated and politicized in the later stages of the Anglo-French Wars, with the growth of a distinctly territorial national identity based on the hexagon and a northern-central French culture. The momentum of legal-bureaucratic incorporation was resumed in the sixteenth century, with the decree of Villers-Cotteret in 1539 making Parisian French the standard language of administration (Lewis 1974; Armstrong 1982, ch. 5; cf. Kantorowicz 1951; Rickard 1974).

In the seventeenth century, strong rulers pursuing policies of cultural standardization and mercantilism created a powerful French state that moulded a growing territorial patriotism. The *grand siècle* also produced a national art, literature, and music which were soon regarded as expressions of the 'genius' of France. In the succeeding century, French writers, critics, and artists called for national regeneration by the state on rational Enlightenment models; and the Revolution itself, with its Jacobin concepts of a civic culture and a unitary French republican nation-state with 'natural frontiers' defended by a citizen army, took these homogenizing drives to their logical conclusion. Only in the nineteenth century did a more genuinely popular French nationalism emerge, one that sought in monarchist-religious or radical-republican myths to shape the destiny of the French nation according to specific visions of 'la France' (Kohn 1967; Weber 1991).

If France is an example of a state-moulded nation, Greece represents a case of a nation formed on the basis of a 'vertical', demotic ethnie. Incorporation of the Greek city-states into the Roman, and Byzantine, empires preserved the Greek language and classical culture as that of the Orthodox Church and lingua franca of the Eastern Mediterranean. Only in the ninth century, when the Latin-speaking provinces had been lost and Greece proper overrun by Slavs and Albanians, did Greek become the language of Court and administration in Constantinople. Hence, language and culture became vehicles for a disrupted Greek continuity, whose ethno-religious identity was heightened by Latin and Islamic Turkish threats in the last years of the Byzantine empire (Ostrogorski 1968; Armstrong 1982, ch. 5).

After 1453, this Greek culture became a unifying focus for all the Greek-speaking communities in Greece proper and the diaspora. The Greek millet, protected and guided by the Orthodox Church and Patriarchate, was recognized as a distinctive ethno-religious community, a people of the Book. But, though Byzantine Orthodoxy preserved a Greek identity, it also hindered it from new political expressions. As a result, those new expressions had to come from outside the Church, from secular diaspora intellectuals like Rhigas Pheraios and Adamantios Korais. Their model likewise was secular and political, the Periclean era of ancient Athens. New strata, the Greek intelligentsia and business class, took the lead in inaugurating a Greek state, under the banner of a secular nationalism that sought its inspiration in classical Greece. Unlike French territorial nationalism which emerged within the crucible of a dynastic French state, Greek demotic nationalism was largely the product of strata and ideals excluded from the political domain; and had therefore to rely far more heavily on vernacular cultures and ethno-historical heritages to create the reality of an ethnic nation (Campbell and Sherrard 1968; Kitromilides 1979).

For the third 'emigrant-colonist' route, the American colonies, founded by immigrants fleeing religious persecution in England and Europe, may serve as example. These Puritan settlements formed a loose ethnie based on common language, customs, and beliefs. For all their divisions, a sense of providential destiny in America sustained the settlers in a new environment. Prior to the War of Independence, an 'ancestral vernacularism' harking back to the Pilgrim Fathers and their Puritan ideals, became an important component in a growing white American identity. This Puritan ideal survived not only the great test of Civil War, but also the massive influx of immigrants in the late nineteenth century. In other 'emigrant-colonist' societies—Australia, Canada (apart from Quebec), South Africa—pioneering settlers have been the main agents of nation formation, with or without assistance from state authorities (Tuveson 1968; Burrows 1982; Seton-Watson 1977, ch. 5).

These three patterns of formation of nations presuppose an ethnic base, and myths of ethnic origins, election, and the golden age. In most cases, we can trace the stages of ethnogenesis, ethnic consolidation, communal decline, and national regeneration, ushering in the era of the modern national state. In some cases, the processes occur over several centuries, in others over a few decades; sometimes, too, the stages may be telescoped or overlap. There is certainly nothing inevitable or irreversible about the transition from ethnie to nation, and it would be a serious misunderstanding of the unpredictability of nationalism to seek to impose some social or cultural law of ethnic evolution on what are often contingent processes.[6]

Nevertheless, it is still possible to isolate some key processes in the formation of most nations. On the one hand, there are the processes of administrative and economic revolution which encourage bureaucratic incorporation by a strong state based on a 'lateral' ethnie. Here the culture of the upper classes of a professionalized ethnic state percolates down to other strata and outwards to peripheral regions and peoples, often through conquest and annexation, as occurred in Britain and France. In this route, the bureaucratic state occupies centre ground and forms the main agent in the

---

[6] By no means all ethnies aspire to transform themselves into nations, nor is the nation a more 'advanced' form of the ethnie, nor must there be a strict one-to-one correspondence between a nation and a particular ethnie. The thesis advanced here is weaker: it states only that (*a*) as a matter of historical fact, the first nations in the modern world (in the West) were constituted on the basis of core ethnies, (*b*) given the prestige of the West in the modern era, other ethnies sought to constitute themselves as nations on this model, (*c*) that those that have not been able to do so, find themselves in great difficulties in their attempts to forge a nation from ethnically heterogenous populations. This is why 'plural' nations require a strong and binding 'civil religion', often based on the heritage of a strategic or dominant ethnie, if they are to unite and survive.

creation of a territorial nation and a bureaucratic nationalism (Citron 1988; A. D. Smith 1986*b*).

In contrast, 'vertical' or demotic ethnies are transformed into ethnic nations through a cultural revolution led by the intelligentsia. This produces a movement of vernacular mobilization of 'the people' by an intelligentsia bent on redis-covering its ethnic heritage. Stranded between tradition and Westernization, native intellectuals seek to resolve their own identity crises by reappropriating the history and culture of their community, or by reconstructing a defective ethno-his-torical record. In the Greek case, the intellectuals leapt over the intervening 2,000 years, and sought a renewed identity for their community in the classical era. Similarly, the Zionist intellectuals rejected two millennia of diaspora persecution to embrace an idealized vision of the biblical past in the land of their forefathers; while Irish intellectuals by-passed their recent tragic past to find in a golden age of Gaelic heroes and Celtic Christianity the model of a modern identity and des-tiny (Kitromilides 1979; Hertzberg 1960; Lyons 1979).

Later, the intelligentsia take up and disseminate these con-cerns, to mobilize a wider social constituency. This they ac-complish by politicizing the culture of the community, making it serve political purposes for which it was never framed. Allied to this is a third familiar process, that of ethnic purification. This begins by seeking to purge the communal culture of foreign elements, and ends by cleansing the com-munity itself of everything alien and extraneous (A. D. Smith 1989).

The 'emigrant-colonist' route appears as a variant of the 'vertical', demotic pattern. But it also differs significantly from it. The main agency of national transformation is uto-pian pioneering settlers who identify with their new environ-ment and preach fulfilment in a promised land fashioned by their labours, often at the expense of indigenous peoples. The new environment encourages in the immigrant colonizers a sense of separate culture and destiny. Linguistic assimilation and local acculturation of newcomers emphasize their differences from the 'mother country', as in Australia, Canada, and Argentina.[7]

Types of modern national community

Inevitably, these three routes to the formation of nations result in rather different kinds of national identity. We may term these types civic, ethnic, and plural nations. These are, of course, ideal types; in practice, given cases include elements from more than one type. Nevertheless, it is useful to distinguish them, if only because they can lead to quite different policies towards minorities and outsiders.

The first, or civic type, familiar to us in Western Europe, emphasizes territorial citizenship. The nation is a *patria*, a fatherland, or land of our fathers. Though there may be a genealogical element, greater emphasis is laid on a historic territory, or homeland, defined by presumed natural frontiers and the bureaucratic state. Residence in the land of the fathers becomes the main criterion of membership of the nation and later of citizenship; residence as opposed to descent. In the civic nation, then, minorities and foreigners can acquire the rights of citizenship through long-standing association, civic loyalty, and participation in a public culture.

Civic nations see themselves as communities of common laws. It is hardly surprising, therefore, that their model is the *polis* of classical antiquity. Rousseau and the neo-classical nationalists of the French Revolution looked back with longing to the civic solidarity and spirit of public self-sacrifice which they saw in republican Rome, Sparta, and Athens. In these *exempla virtutis*, they found that unity of collective purpose which comes from a shared civil religion and culture,

---

[7] The situation in Latin America was, and is, rather different. The 'emigrant-colonists' were not fleeing (or being expelled from) Europe, and they intermarried with much larger indigenous peoples with often advanced civilizations, whom they subjugated and proselytized. Nevertheless, creole élites too became distanced from Spain and Portugal and sought a separate collective destiny in a new environment based on a *mestizo* culture (see Masur 1966).

one that rested securely on common values, customs, myths, and memories (Cobban 1964; Rosenblum 1967).

In contrast, ethnic nations emphasize collective ties of descent. Individuals are members of an ethnic nation only in so far as they regard themselves and are regarded by others as descendants of the original, or founding, generations of the community, and share common origins in time and place. It matters not a whit that such ancestors and origins are more fictive than real. A myth of common origins and descent has been elevated into the defining criterion of the nation itself. Hence the need to designate ethnic members and contrast them with non-members who do not share in the defining myth, even though they may be long-standing residents; and where appropriate to exclude and cleanse the body of the nation from contamination by such outsiders. Ethnic purification is built into the logic of genealogically defined nations (see Mosse 1964).[8]

Ethnic nations also display a fervent commitment to vernacular culture and ethno-history. Acquisition of that culture and history becomes a political obligation for every member, a test of 'true descent' and collective loyalty. This is the legacy of the demotic ethnie, with its sharply delineated boundaries and cross-class culture. But it is also the result of the long struggles for recognition that so many of the smaller ethnies had to wage, and the role that mass mobilization by a returning intelligentsia played in this struggle. When Finns and Czechs, Basques and Armenians broke loose from the states in which they had so long been incorporated, their intelligentsias had to appeal to the people as a whole through a rediscovered vernacular culture, to challenge the state and recast the political map (Jutikkala 1962; Pech 1976; Walker 1980; Conversi 1990).

[8] We should not, however, confuse ethnic nationalism with racism, nor the ethnie with 'race'. The basis of the former is cultural, the belief that communities are culturally and historically unique symbolized by a myth of (often fictive) common descent. The basis of the latter is alleged physical characteristics and biological descent, buttressed by hierarchical power relationships (see Van den Berghe 1967; Jenkins 1986).

In the third type, the plural nation, residence and ethnic descent are subordinated, at least in theory, to an overarching civic religion. At the same time, the state makes provision for institutional ethnic cultures. The nation is composed of a series of quite diverse immigrant part-ethnies which retain elements of their original cultures, adapted to the new setting; but individuals give their primary allegiance to a public, mass culture. They are Australians, Americans, Argentinians first, and Irish, Germans, or Jews thereafter.

In practice, the public culture of these 'plural' nations is very much the legacy of the original dominant pioneer culture. The English settlers in Australia, America, and Canada (apart from Quebec) dictated cultural development, just as they dominated society and politics, well before any influx of other ethnic settlers; and their descendants' culture continues to define the language, the symbols, and ceremonies, and the legal order of the new plural nation of immigrant settlers.

These three ideal-types of national identity have been forged out of different patterns of formation of the nation. Actual nations frequently mingle elements from each of the types. But the types serve to remind us that nationalism is not all 'one thing', that there are divergent national experiences and therefore very different nationalist policies. This is of particular relevance to the vexed question of citizenship. Differences between the three kinds of national identity are reflected in contrasting policies over minorities and immigration. Similarly attempts to move from one type of identity to another are mirrored in those policies. As the present situation in France and Germany suggests, such attempts have not always met with success; public policies and popular attitudes may well remain out of step.

Conclusion

It has to be said that the prognosis for civic and plural types of the nation superseding ethno-national identities is not hopeful. The last few years have witnessed a veritable explosion of nationalisms demanding the creation or recreation of specifically ethnic nations on the basis of demotic ethnies. While we should not allow ourselves to be carried away by the excitements of the moment, it would be a serious error to dismiss present, or future, waves of ethnic nationalism as somehow secondary to the great movements of modern history. The history of the modern world since the French Revolution has witnessed repeated explosions of ethnic protest and ethnic nationalism in various parts of the globe, and it would be foolhardy to predict an early end to either. Like it or not, the nation remains the major actor in world affairs and the main carrier of social and political development; and ethnicity continues to be the major source of mass mobilization (Hobsbawm 1990, ch. 6; A. D. Smith 1990).

As we have seen, modern national identities are not the products of recent developments and revolutions alone. They depend on various kinds of pre-modern ethnic cores and are shaped by different routes and agents of national transformation, often over long periods. This means that without the initial networks of ethnic ties underpinning the competition of states, modern capitalism, bureaucracy, and communications could not have conjured into being the world of nations that we know. The processes of forging national identity can often be traced back for several centuries. Even where these are of more recent origin, pre-existing ethnic ties and sentiments, myths and memories, symbols and traditions provide fertile soil for bureaucrats, intelligentsias, or others to plant the national idea and bring it to fruition.

It follows then that the nationalisms with which we must all come to terms today stem from older and deeper roots than many of us envisaged. With such deep foundations, national identities are unlikely to wither away or be easily transmuted into higher order political unions. We shall have to make our peace with ethnic identity and nationalism and build on the international order as we find it today, or risk continual frustration and disillusionment.

REFERENCES

ABRAMS, DOMINIC, and HOGG, MICHAEL A. (1990) (eds.), *Social Identity Theory* (Hemel Hempstead: Harvester).

ARMSTRONG, J. (1982), *Nations before Nationalism* (Chapel Hill, NC: University of North Carolina Press).

ATIYAH, A. S. (1968), *A History of Eastern Christianity* (London: Methuen).

AUSTEN, JANE (1990), *Emma*, ed. James Kinsley, The World's Classics (Oxford: Oxford University Press).

BALSDON, J. V. P. (1979), *Romans and Aliens* (London: Duckworth).

BARZUN, J. (1932), *The French Race: Theories of its Origins and their Social and Political Implications Prior to the Revolution* (New York: Columbia University Press).

BELL, A. P., and WEINBERG, S. (1978), *Homosexualities: A Study of Diversity among Men and Women* (New York: Simon and Schuster).

BELL, D. (1975), 'Ethnicity and social change', in N. Glazer and D. Moynihan (eds.), *Ethnicity: Theory and Experience* (Cambridge, Mass.: Harvard University Press), 141–74.

BENSTOCK, SHARI (1988) (ed.), *The Private Self: Theory and Practice of Women's Autobiographical Writing* (Chapel Hill, NC: University of North Carolina Press).

BORST, C. V. (1970) (ed.), *The Mind-Brain Identity Theory* (London: Macmillan).

BOSWELL, J. (1980), *Christianity, Social Tolerance, and Homosexuality* (Chicago: University of Chicago Press).

—— (1982), 'Revolutions, universals and sexual categories', *Salmagundi*, 58–9: 89–113.

BRANCH, M. (1985) (ed.), *Kalevala: The Land of Heroes*, trans. W. F. Kirby (London: Athlone Press).

References

BRASS, P. (1979), 'Elite groups, symbol manipulation and ethnic identity among the Muslims of South Asia', in M. Yapp and D. Taylor (eds.), *Political Identity in South Asia* (London: Curzon Press), 35–77.

BROCK, P. (1976), *The Slovak National Awakening* (Toronto: University of Toronto Press).

BROOKS, PETER (1984), *Reading for the Plot* (New York: Alfred Knopf).

BRUNER, JEROME (1991), 'The narrative construction of reality', *Critical Inquiry*, 18/1: 1–21.

BURROWS, E. G. (1982), 'Bold forefathers and the cruel step-mother: ideologies of descent in the American Revolution', unpub. paper for Conference on Legitimation by Descent, Maison des Sciences de l'Homme, Paris.

CAMPBELL, J., and SHERRARD, P. (1968), *Modern Greece* (London: Benn).

CARRAS, C. (1983), *3,000 Years of Greek Identity: Myth or Reality?* (Athens: Domus Books).

CAVE, TERENCE (1988), *Recognitions: A Study in Poetics* (Oxford: Clarendon Press; paperback repr. 1990).

CITRON, S. (1988), *Le Mythe national* (Paris: Presses Ouvriers).

COBBAN, A. (1964), *Rousseau and the Modern State* (2nd edn., London: Allen and Unwin).

COLLINS, STEVEN (1982), *Selfless Persons* (Cambridge: Cambridge University Press).

CONNOR, W. (1978), 'A nation is a nation, is a state, is an ethnic group, is a . . .', *Ethnic and Racial Studies*, 1/4: 378–400.

—— (1990), 'When is a nation?', *Ethnic and Racial Studies*, 13/1: 92–103.

CONVERSI, D. (1990), 'Language or race? The choice of core values in the development of Catalan and Basque nationalisms', *Ethnic and Racial Studies*, 13/1: 50–70.

CORRIGAN, P., and SAYER, D. (1985), *The Great Arch: English State Formation as Cultural Revolution* (Oxford: Blackwell).

DAHLSTROM, W. G., and WELSH, G. S. (1960), *An MMPI Handbook: A Guide to Use in Clinical Practice and Research* (Minneapolis: University of Minnesota Press).

DANCY, JONATHAN (forthcoming) (ed.), *Derek Parfit and his Critics* (Oxford: Blackwell).

DARWIN, CHARLES (1871), *Descent of Man* (London: John Murray).

156

References

DAVIDSON, A. (1987), 'Sex and the emergence of sexuality', *Critical Inquiry*, 14: 16–48; repr. in Stein 1992: 89–132.

DE BEAUVOIR, S. (1953), *The Second Sex* (New York: Knopf).

DENNIS, NIGEL (1955), *Cards of Identity* (London: Weidenfeld and Nicolson).

DÖRNER, G. (1976), *Hormones and Brain Differentiation* (Amsterdam: Elsevier).

DOVER, K. J. (1978), *Greek Homosexuality* (Cambridge, Mass.: Harvard University Press).

DYNES, W. (1988), 'Wrestling with the social boa constructor', *Out in Academia*, 2: 18–29; repr. in Stein 1992: 209–38.

EISENSTEIN-BARZILAY, I. (1959), 'National and anti-national trends in the Berlin Haskalah', *Jewish Social Studies*, 21: 165–92.

ELIOT, GEORGE (1988), *Daniel Deronda*, ed. Graham Handley, The World's Classics (Oxford: Oxford University Press).

ERDINAST-VULCAN, DAPHNA (1991), *Joseph Conrad and the Modern Temper* (Oxford: Clarendon Press).

FARHNI, D. (1983), *An Outline History of Switzerland: From the Origins to the Present Day* (Zurich: Pro Helvetia).

FEIGL, H. (1953), 'The mind-body problem in the development of logical empiricism', in H. Feigl and M. Brodbeck (eds.), *Readings in the Philosophy of Science* (New York: Appleton-Century-Crofts), 622.

FISHMAN, J. (1980), 'Social theory and ethnography: neglected perspectives on language and ethnicity in Eastern Europe', in P. Sugar (ed.), *Ethnic Diversity and Conflict in Eastern Europe* (Santa Barbara, Calif.: ABC-Clio), 69–99.

FOUCAULT, M. (1978), *The History of Sexuality* (New York: Random House); repr. (in part) in Stein 1992: 11–23.

FREUD, SIGMUND (1905), *Three Essays on the Theory of Sexuality*, in J. Strachey (ed.), *Collected Works of Freud* (London: Hogarth, 1953), vii. 125–243.

GEERTZ, C. (1963), 'The integrative revolution', in C. Geertz (ed.), *Old Societies and New States* (New York: Free Press).

GOULD, S. J. (1977), *Ever Since Darwin* (New York: Norton).

GOY, R. W., WOLF, J. E., and EISELE, S. G. (1977), 'Experimental female hermaphroditism in rhesus monkeys: anatomical and psychological characteristics', in J. Money and H. Mustaph (eds.), *Handbook of Sexology* (New York: Elsevier), 139–56.

References

GREEN, R. (1974), *Sexual Identity Conflict in Children and Adults* (New York: Basic Books).

GROSBY, S. (1991), 'Religion and nationality in antiquity: the worship of Yahweh and ancient Israel', *European Journal of Sociology*, 32: 229–65.

HACKING, I. (1986), 'Making up people', in T. Heller, M. Sosna, and D. Wellbery (eds.), *Reconstructing Individualism: Autonomy, Individuality, and the Self in Western Thought* (Stanford, Calif.: Stanford University Press); repr. in Stein 1992: 69–88.

HAMILTON, W. D., AXELROD, R., and TANESE, R. (1990), 'Sexual reproduction as an adaptation to resist parasites (a review), *Proc. Nat. Acad. Sci. USA*, 87: 3566–73.

HERTZ, F. (1944), *Nationality in History and Politics* (London: Routledge and Kegan Paul).

HERTZBERG, A. (1960) (ed.), *The Zionist Idea: A Reader* (New York: Meridian Books).

HOBSBAWM, E. (1990), *Nations and Nationalism Since 1780* (Cambridge: Cambridge University Press).

HOROWITZ, D. (1985), *Ethnic Groups in Conflict* (Berkeley, Calif.: University of California Press).

HOWE, N. (1989), *Migration and Mythmaking in Anglo-Saxon England* (New Haven, Conn.: Yale University Press).

HUGHES, A. L. (1988), *Evolution and Human Kinship* (Oxford: Oxford University Press).

HUTCHINSON, J. (1987), *The Dynamics of Cultural Nationalism: The Gaelic Revival and the Creation of the Irish Nation State* (London: Allen and Unwin).

IM HOF, U. (1991), *Mythos Schweiz: Identität—Nation—Geschichte, 1291–1991* (Zurich: Neue Zürcher Verlag).

JAMES, HENRY (1876), '*Daniel Deronda*: A Conversation', *Atlantic Monthly*, 38 (Dec.): 684–94.

JENKINS, R. (1986), 'Social anthropological models of interethnic relation', in J. Rex and D. Mason (eds.), *Theories of Race and Ethnic Relations* (Cambridge: Cambridge University Press), 170–86.

JOHNSON, BARBARA (1993) (ed.), *Freedom and Interpretation: The Oxford Amnesty Lectures 1992* (New York: Basic Books).

JUST, R. (1989), 'Triumph of the Ethnos', in E. Tonkin, M. McDonald, and M. Chapman (eds.), *History and Ethnicity*, ASA Monographs 27 (New York: Routledge).

JUTIKKALA, E. (1962), *A History of Finland* (London: Thames and Hudson), 71–88.

KANTOROWICZ, E. H. (1951), 'Pro Patria Mori in medieval political thought', *American Historical Review*, 56: 472–92.

KEDOURIE, E. (1960), *Nationalism* (London: Hutchinson).

—— (1971) (ed.), *Nationalism in Asia and Africa* (London: Weidenfeld and Nicolson).

KENNY, A. J. P. (1989), *The Metaphysics of Mind* (Oxford: Clarendon Press), 30.

KERMODE, FRANK (1973), *The Sense of an Ending: Studies in the Theory of Fiction* (London: Oxford University Press; first pub. 1967).

KINSEY, A. C., POMEROY, W. B., and MARTIN, C. E. (1948), *Sexual Behavior in the Human Male* (Philadelphia: W. B. Saunders).

—— —— —— and GEBHARD, P. H. (1953), *Sexual Behavior in the Human Female* (Philadelphia: W. B. Saunders).

KITROMILIDES, P. (1979), 'The dialectic of intolerance: ideological dimensions of ethnic conflict', *Journal of the Hellenic Diaspora*, 6/4: 5–30.

—— (1989), '"Imagined Communities" and the origins of the national question in the Balkans', *European History Quarterly*, 19/2: 149–92.

KOHN, H. (1940), 'The origins of English nationalism', *Journal of the History of Ideas*, 1: 69–94.

—— (1957), *Nationalism and Liberty: The Swiss Example* (New York: Macmillan).

—— (1967), *Prelude to Nation-States: The French and German Experience, 1789–1815* (New York: Van Nostrand).

KREJCI, J. (1979), 'Ethnic problems in Europe', in S. Giner and M. S. Archer (eds.), *Contemporary Europe, Social Structures and Cultural Patterns* (London: Routledge and Kegan Paul).

—— and VELIMSKY, V. (1981), *Ethnic and Political Nations in Europe* (London: Croom Helm).

KRIPKE, S. (1979), 'Identity and necessity', first pub. 1971, repr. in T. Honderich and M. Burnyeat (eds.), *Philosophy as it is* (Harmondsworth: Penguin), 478–513.

LEAVIS, F. R. (1948), *The Great Tradition: George Eliot, Henry James, and Joseph Conrad* (London: George W. Stewart).

LEHMANN, J.-P. (1982), *The Roots of Modern Japan* (London: Macmillan).

LEWIS, A. (1974), *Knights and Samurai* (London: Temple Smith).

LYONS, F. S. (1979), *Culture and Anarchy in Ireland, 1890–1930* (London: Oxford University Press).

McCULLEY, B. T. (1966), *English Education and the Origins of Indian Nationalism* (Gloucester, Mass.: Smith).

MacDOUGALL, H. (1982), *Racial Myth in English History: Trojans, Teutons and Anglo-Saxons* (Montreal: Harvest House; Hanover, NH: University Press of New England).

McINTOSH, M. (1968), 'The homosexual role', *Social Problems*, 16: 182–92.

MacINTYRE, ALASDAIR (1985), *After Virtue* (London: Duckworth; first edn. 1981).

MACKIE, JOHN (1976), *Problems from Locke* (Oxford: Oxford University Press).

MASTERS, W. H., and JOHNSON, V. E. (1966), *Human Sexual Response* (Boston: Little, Brown).

MASUR, G. (1966), *Nationalism in Latin America* (New York: Macmillan).

MONEY, J. (1961), 'Sex hormones and other variables in human eroticism', in W. C. Young (ed.), *Sex and Internal Secretions*, 3rd edn. (Baltimore: Williams and Wilkins), 1383–1400.

—— and EHRHARDT, A. (1972), *Man and Woman: Boy and Girl* (Baltimore: Johns Hopkins University Press).

—— and SCHWARTZ, M. (1978), 'Biosocial determinants of gender identity differentiation and development', in J. B. Hutchinson (ed.), *Biological Determinants of Sexual Behavior* (New York: Wiley), 765–84.

MOSSE, G. (1964), *The Crisis of German Ideology* (New York: Grosset and Dunlap).

NAGEL, THOMAS (1970), 'Physicalism', in Borst 1970: 214–30.

—— (1986), *The View from Nowhere* (Oxford: Oxford University Press).

NAIRN, T. (1977), *The Break-up of Britain* (London: New Left Books).

NEUSNER, J. (1981), *Max Weber Revisited: Religion and Society in Ancient Judaism* (Oxford: Oxford Centre for Postgraduate Hebrew Studies).

NOZICK, ROBERT (1981), *Philosophical Explanations* (Cambridge, Mass.: Harvard University Press).

OKAMURA, J. (1981), 'Situational ethnicity', *Ethnic and Racial Studies*, 4/4: 452–65.

References

OSTROGORSKI, G. (1968), *History of the Byzantine State* (Oxford: Basil Blackwell).

PADGUG, R. (1979), 'Sexual matters: on conceptualizing sexuality in history', *Radical History Review*, 20: 3–23; repr. in Stein 1992: 43–67.

PARFIT, D. (1984), *Reasons and Persons* (Oxford: Oxford University Press).

—— (1986), *Reasons and Persons* (2nd edn., Oxford: Oxford University Press), 245–66.

PASCAL, BLAISE (1963), *Pensées*, in *Œuvres complètes*, ed. Louis Lafuma (Paris: Éditions du Seuil).

PECH, S. (1976), 'The nationalist movements of the Austrian Slavs', *Social History*, 9: 336–56.

PEEL, J. (1989), 'The cultural work of Yoruba ethnogenesis', in E. Tonkin, M. MacDonald, and M. Chapman (eds.), *History and Ethnicity* (London: Routledge), 198–215.

PERRY, JOHN (1975) (ed.), *Personal Identity* (Berkeley, Calif.: University of California Press).

PLACE, U. T. (1970), 'Materialism as a scientific hypothesis', in Borst 1970: 83–6.

QUINE, W. V. (1987), *Quiddities* (Cambridge, Mass.: Harvard University Press), 89–92.

QUINTON, A. (1975), 'The soul', in J. Perry (ed.), *Personal Identity* (Berkeley, Calif.: University of California Press), 60.

RADO, S. (1940), 'A critical examination of the concept of bisexuality', *Psychosomatic Medicine*, 2: 459–67.

RENAN, E. (1882), *Qu'est-ce que la nation?* (Paris: Calmann Levy).

REYNOLDS, S. (1983), 'Medieval *origines gentium* and the community of the realm', *History*, 68: 375–90.

—— (1984), *Kingdoms and Communities in Western Europe, 900–1300* (Oxford: Clarendon).

RICKARD, P. (1974), *A History of the French Language* (London: Hutchinson University Library).

RICŒUR, PAUL (1992), *Oneself as Another*, trans. Kathleen Blamey (Chicago: University of Chicago Press; orig. French edn. 1990).

ROSDOLSKY, R. (1964), 'Friedrich Engels und das Problem der "Geschichtslosen Völker"', *Archiv für Sozialgeschichte*, 4: 87–282.

ROSENBLUM, R. (1967), *Transformations in Late Eighteenth Century Art* (Princeton, NJ: Princeton University Press).

References

RUSE, M. (1982), *Darwinism Defended: A Guide to the Evolution Controversies* (Reading, Mass.: Addison-Wesley).

—— (1988), *Homosexuality: A Philosophical Perspective* (Oxford: Blackwell).

RUSTOW, D. (1967), *A World of Nations* (Washington, DC: Brookings Institution).

SAGHIR, M. T., and ROBBINS, E. (1973), *Male and Female Homosexuality: A Comprehensive Investigation* (Baltimore: Williams and Wilkins).

SAMUEL, R. (1989) (ed.), *Patriotism, the Making and Unmaking of British National Identity*, 3 vols. (London: Routledge).

SCHERMERHORN, R. (1970), *Comparative Ethnic Relations* (New York: Random House).

SCHEUCH, E. K. (1966), 'Cross-national comparisons with aggregate data', in R. Merrit and S. Rokkan (eds.), *Comparing Nations* (New Haven, Conn.: Yale University Press).

SETON-WATSON, H. (1977), *Nations and States* (London: Methuen).

SHAFFER, J. (1970), 'Could mental states be brain processes?', in Borst 1970: 113–22.

SMITH, A. D. (1979), *Nationalism in the Twentieth Century* (Oxford: Martin Robertson).

—— (1983), *Theories of Nationalism* (2nd edn., London: Duckworth; 1st edn. 1971).

—— (1984a), 'National identity and myths of ethnic descent', *Research in Social Movements, Conflict and Change*, 7: 95–130.

—— (1984b), 'Ethnic myths and ethnic revivals', *European Journal of Sociology*, 25: 283–305.

—— (1986a), *The Ethnic Origins of Nations* (Oxford: Blackwell).

—— (1986b), 'State-making and nation-building', in J. Hall (ed.), *States in History* (Oxford: Blackwell), 228–63.

—— (1988), 'The myth of the "modern nation" and the myths of nations', *Ethnic and Racial Studies*, 11/1: 1–26.

—— (1989), 'The origins of nations', *Ethnic and Racial Studies*, 12/3: 340–67.

—— (1990), 'The supersession of nationalism?', *International Journal of Comparative Sociology*, 31/1–2: 1–31.

—— (1991), *National Identity* (Harmondsworth: Penguin).

—— (1992), 'Chosen peoples: why ethnic groups survive', *Ethnic and Racial Studies*, 15/3: 436–56.

References

SMITH, L. (1984) (ed.), *The Making of Britain: The Dark Ages* (London: Macmillan).

STACK, J. F. (1986) (ed.), *The Primordial Challenge: Ethnicity in the Contemporary World* (New York: Greenwood Press).

STCHERBATSKY, THEODORE (1919), 'The Soul Theory of the Buddhists', *Bulletin de l'Académie de Science de Russie*, 845.

STEIN, E. (1992) (ed.), *Forms of Desire: Sexual Orientation and the Social Constructionist Controversy* (New York: Routledge).

STOLLER, R. (1968), *Sex and Gender: On the Development of Masculinity and Femininity* (New York: Science House).

STRAWSON, P. F. (1990), *Individuals: An Essay in Descriptive Metaphysics* (London: Routledge; first pub. 1959).

SYMONS, D. (1979), *The Evolution of Human Sexuality* (New York: Oxford University Press).

TAYLOR, CHARLES (1992), *Sources of the Self: The Making of Modern Identity* (Cambridge: Cambridge University Press; first pub. 1989).

THADEN, E. C. (1964), *Conservative Nationalism in Nineteenth Century Russia* (Seattle: University of Washington Press).

TILLY, C. (1975) (ed.), *The Formation of National States in Western Europe* (Princeton, NJ: Princeton University Press).

TIPTON, L. (1972) (ed.), *Nationalism in the Middle Ages* (New York: Holt, Rinehart and Winston).

TIVEY, L. (1980) (ed.), *The Nation-State* (Oxford: Martin Robertson).

TRIGGER, B. G., KEMP, B. J., O'CONNOR, D., and LLOYD, A. B. (1983), *Ancient Egypt: A Social History* (Cambridge: Cambridge University Press).

TUDOR, H. (1972), *Political Myth* (London: Pall Mall Press/ Macmillan).

TUVESON, E. L. (1968), *Redeemer Nation: The Idea of America's Millenial Role* (Chicago: University of Chicago Press).

VAN DEN BERGHE, P. (1967), *Race and Racism* (New York: Wiley).

VARGHA-KHADEM, F., O'GORMAN, A. M., and WATTERS, G. V. (1985), 'Aphasia and handedness in relation to hemispheric side, age at injury and severity of cerebral lesion during childhood', *Brain*, 108: 677–96.

WALKER, C. (1980), *Armenia: The Survival of a Nation* (London: Routledge).

References

WEBER, E. (1991), *My France: Politics, Culture, Myth* (Cambridge, Mass.: Belknap Press of Harvard University Press).

WEEKS, J. (1977), *Coming out: Homosexual Politics in Britain, from the Nineteenth Century to the Present* (London: Quartet).

WELCH, C. (1966), *Dreams of Unity: Pan-Africanism and Political Unification in West Africa* (Ithaca, NY: Cornell University Press).

WIGGINS, DAVID (1967), *Identity and Spatio-temporal Continuity* (Oxford: Basil Blackwell), 50.

—— (1980), *Sameness and Substance* (Oxford: Blackwell).

WILLIAMS, BERNARD (1991), *Problems of the Self: Philosophical Papers 1956–1972* (Cambridge: Cambridge University Press; first pub. 1973).

WILLIAMS, G. C. (1975), *Sex and Evolution* (Princeton, NJ: Princeton University Press).

WISEMAN, D. J. (1973) (ed.), *Peoples of the Old Testament* (Oxford: Oxford University Press).

ZERNATTO, G. (1944), 'Nation: the history of a word', *Review of Politics*, 6: 351–66.

INDEX

Index

Index

identity 5–6, 7
Hobsbawm, E. 139 n. 5
homosexuality 74–8
  and cross-gender features
    79–81, 88
  determinants vi, 79, 81–8
  and identity 97–8
  incidence 77 n. 1, 79
  and ontology 91–7
  as social construct vi, 88–91,
    92–8
  and transsexuality 72
hormones:
  and sex 67, 70
  and sexual orientation 83–8, 89

identity, collective, *see* identity,
  social
identity, cultural 130–2
identity, ethnic 123–4
  and national identity 132–6
identity, fictional vi, 8, 99–127
  and impacted identity 115–19,
    125
  and inward turn 104–9
  and narrative 109–13, 116–19,
    126–7
  and philosophical fiction 99–102
  and recognition plot 113–15,
    116, 118, 120–3
  and textual identity 102–4
identity, group, *see* identity, social
identity, national vi, 129–53
  and collective cultural identity
    130–2
  ethnic bases 136–41
  and ethnic identity 132–6
  and modern national community
    150–2
  and nation formation 141–50
identity, numerical v, 1–11, 13–14
  Best Candidate Theory 6–7
  and continuity 4–5, 14
  as indeterminate v, 34
  and one/many 2–4
  and part/whole 4
  type and particular 7–9
identity, personal v–vi, 13–45,

  47–63
  Arguments from Above/Below
    29–32, 39
  and beliefs 15–16, 27–8, 41–2, 45
  and Best Candidate Theory 6–7
  Brain-Based Criterion 38–43,
    115–16
  as determinate 15–16, 22–3
  and group 105–8, 117–18,
    119–22, 130
  and inward turn 104–9
  and language 11, 19–20, 24–6,
    32–7, 39–41, 52–3
  and mind/brain identity 49–54
  nature 13–28
  Physical/Bodily Criterion
    14–15, 33–7, 115–16
  and physiology of brain 56–9
  Psychological Criterion 15, 37–8
  and reductionism 16–18, 19–20,
    22, 26–7, 30–3, 45
  and the self 99–100, 104–9
  significance 28–45
  and textual identity 102–4
identity, qualitative v, 13–14, 47–8
identity, sexual vi, 10, 65–98
  and aetiology 81–8
  and bisexuality 78–81
  and gender identity 72–4, 79, 98
  and homosexual identity 97–8
  and ontology 92–7
  and sex 66–71
  and sexual orientation 10, 74–8
  as social construct 65, 88–91,
    92–8
identity, social 2, 7, 129
  constructed 8
  and cultural identity 131
  and personal identity 8, 105–8,
    117–19, 120–2, 130
  shared 7–9
individual:
  and cultural identity 130
  and ethnic nation 151
  and numerical identity 3
  and politics of identity 10–11
  and social identity 8–9, 106–9,
    117–18, 119–22

Index

Index compiled by Meg Davies